Herbs of the Southern Shaman

Another fine book from the always-interesting pen of Steve Andrews. Concise, knowledgeable, clearly and distinctly written, it can be enjoyed on many levels: as a reference book, a spiritual guide, a horticultural manual, or simply for entertainment. A welcome addition to any ethnobotanists library.
C. J. Stone, author and journalist

The Bard of Ely's deep delve into the shamanistic properties of the herbs of this world's southern hemisphere is a triumph. Where to find your sample, what you do with it, and more importantly what happens next are all covered in fine and easy to understand detail. A psychonautist's Rosetta Stone.
Peter Finch, poet and author

Once again, Steve Andrews manages a mix of fact, fantastic detail, wise reflection, and unique insight in order to enlighten us about the herbs of South and Central America, their histories, properties, uses, and influences upon the modern world. This timely tome is as entertaining as it is educational; as thought-provoking as it is thorough. The style is clear, engaging, and accessible, whilst the subject matters remains crisp, sharp, and intelligent. A well-written, well-researched book that deserves to be widely read, *Herbs of the Southern Shaman* is undoubtedly set to become a classic. I enjoyed the book immensely.
Mab Jones, writer and poet

As a practicing 'white witch' and lover of plants and nature, I found Steve Andrew's book *Herbs of the Northern Shaman* invaluable. Clearly written and beautifully illustrated with detailed photographs that help identify the plants, I can't wait for a 'Southern' version to come out as a reference and companion on my globe trotting adventures.

Carli Susu

Herbs of the Southern Shaman

Also by Steve Andrews

Pagan Portals - Herbs of the Sun, Moon and Planets

Herbs of the Northern Shaman

Herbs of the Southern Shaman

Steve Andrews

Winchester, UK
Washington, USA

First published by Moon Books, 2019
Moon Books is an imprint of John Hunt Publishing Ltd., No. 3 East Street, Alresford
Hampshire SO24 9EE, UK
office1@jhpbooks.net
www.johnhuntpublishing.com
www.moon-books.net

For distributor details and how to order please visit the 'Ordering' section on our website.

Text copyright: Steve Andrews 2018

ISBN: 978 1 78904 099 9
978 1 78904 100 2 (ebook)
Library of Congress Control Number: 2018940513

A CIP catalogue record for this book is available from the British Library.

Design: Stuart Davies

UK: Printed and bound by CPI Group (UK) Ltd, Croydon, CR0 4YY
US: Printed and bound by Thomson Shore, 7300 West Joy Road, Dexter, MI 48130

We operate a distinctive and ethical publishing philosophy in
all areas of our business, from our global network of authors to
production and worldwide distribution.

Contents

Shamanism is not a religion, it is a set of techniques and the principal technique is the use of psychedelic plants.
Terence Mckenna, (1946–2000)

Acknowledgements

First of all, I wish to thank Tim Brett and Iolo Jones for their help with photos. Much gratitude also goes to Aziz Ipsule for providing black-and-white illustrations, and I have also used one by the late Janice Pugsley. Plenty more thanks go to all the enterprising people out there, who are responsible for some excellent ethnobotanical websites. Especial gratitude goes to Torsten Wiedemann of Shaman Australis Botanicals. Torsten very kindly gave permission for the republishing of short extracts from his work. Even more gratitude to Daniel Siebert and to Greendrag, who I am indebted to for allowing me to reproduce the entire contents of 'A New Awareness Through Salvia' – a personal account of experiences with the herb. And also, to John W. Allen aka 'Mushroom John', for personally directing me to some of his theories and research findings on several mushroom species. Further thanks go to Lucius of TAC Ethnobotanicals for his encouraging correspondence and information, to Dan of the sadly defunct Gnostic Garden, to the splendid Erowid Psychoactive Vaults and the Lycaeum for being there for consultation. To Carol Ann Wells and everyone at Stain Blue website, for info on the mushrooms that have that effect amongst others, to Forbidden Fruit and Spirit Plants for their forums and the contacts I have made through them, and to the late Elizabeth Gips, who made her name not only as an author and DJ who was still working in her 80s, but as the 'Haight Ashbury Pilgrim'. Elizabeth was behind me all the way. I am also very grateful for the general support and assistance of my late father Bill Andrews. I must also thank Chris Allan of Abbey Ethnobotanicals for his last minute assistance with some technical information, as well as offering to help with future projects. I am grateful to all the writers I have quoted from, and all the shamans, thanks, too to anyone I have forgotten here –

please forgive me, and I hope you will find yourself included and credited elsewhere in this book. Finally, my gratitude goes out once again to my past publishers at Loompanics Unlimited, and to Moon Books my current publishers, for helping me make this happen.

Foreword

Following on from my book *Herbs of the Northern Shaman*, I felt that a sequel should be written to detail the wealth of herbs that can be described as entheogens that come from the southern hemisphere, and the more southerly parts of the north. I had considered writing a book to cover the middle zone and equatorial regions because Central America has a large proportion of herbs that can be used for shamanic purposes. It is a bit tricky trying to decide what falls within this middle zone and some countries at the top of South America are definitely considered as being in the south. I finally settled on calling this book *Herbs of the Southern Shaman*.

Of course, Mother Nature is not to be bounded by our unnatural divisions and boundaries between countries and territories. So many herbs grow wherever they can take root and flourish.

For some reason, Mexico, in particular, and Central America, as already noted, appears to have more species of psychoactive herbs that can be used shamanically than anywhere else on the planet. This has meant that many American Indian cultures have been very strongly influenced by these plants and the use of such herbs has been widespread among the shamans of the many tribes for thousands of years. The remaining architecture and cultural artefacts of great civilisations like the Incas, the Aztecs and the Mayan Indians often depict sacred 'power plants' like the morning glory, the datura and the magic mushroom amongst their iconography and symbolism. In fact, the Aztecs had a semi-divine figure known as Xochipilli, which translated means 'Prince of Flowers', and his statue is adorned with many stylized glyphs depicting sacred shamanic herbs. It is easy to conjecture that these people believed that this prince ruled over the hallucinogenic plants he is shown with, or maybe that he derived his magical powers from them. We can tell from many such sources that these herbs were used in religious rituals and ceremonies. The use of entheogenic herbs has been carried on and practised still by the shamans and neo-shamans of today.

Some of these shamans have become famous for their knowledge and skills in practising shamanism and herbal medicine, people like Maria Sabina of the Mazatec Indians of Mexico, who is featured in many books about these subjects.

The knowledge of such plants and their cultivation and use has often spread far from the original source and is happening now with the worldwide interest being shown in ethnobotanical plants and shamanism. *Salvia divinorum* the diviner's mint, for example, as far as we know originated in Mexico, but it has since been propagated on the other side of the globe. Many other species like the morning glory have proved so popular with gardeners that the plants are grown worldwide wherever it is warm enough. Others have territories that extend and overlap within countries in the northern and southern hemispheres.

I wish to point out that were it not for Dr. Richard Evan Schultes and Dr. Albert Hoffmann's ground-breaking ethnobotanical classic – *Plants of the Gods* – much of the information we currently have, would I fear, not be available for examination and debate. All authors on these subjects clearly owe them a great debt. However, whilst researching for this my own book, I became acutely aware of how many writers have merely re-written and recycled the information from this past masterpiece about entheogens. Sometimes it can be difficult to find fresh material. Often nothing new is added and nothing questioned. If possible, I have tried to break this mould, whilst still acknowledging our debt to these and other ethnobotanical scholars and pioneers.

I also wish to state that the purpose of this work is for educational reasons and to provide horticultural and botanical information for consideration. Even though I have included personal descriptions of hallucinogenic experiences by users

2

of some of the plants detailed in this work, I am in no way advocating the ingestion or use of any of these herbs, many of which are very poisonous when consumed and can present a very real danger. It will be pointed out in the text when a species is particularly toxic, and I also wish make it clear that the shamans of the cultures that use these plants often obey very strict dieting and other rules and regulations when they partake of sacred herbal preparations. Often, these rules have been formulated after countless years of hard-won experience for particular tribes and there is a very good reason for them. For example, the herbal mixtures that make up the brew known as ayahuasca are only safely consumed when dietary restrictions are followed. Many of the peoples that used these herbs treated them as religious sacraments, as 'teachers', to help divine something, or maybe to treat an illness. The idea of taking such plants for fun and recreational purposes would have had no place in their understanding of the world. The laws relating to supply, possession, cultivation and use of many of these herbs varies from one year to the next and is different in one country to another. The reader is advised to be aware of this and to find out the laws that apply in the lands that he or she may be in. Neither the author or publisher are condoning breaking the law, and neither do they accept any responsibility for harm resulting from the unwise or incorrect usage of such herbs as those described in this book.

I intend showing medicinal uses of herbs described and also, if I can find the information, details of astrological planetary rulers and associated deities as well as magical properties assigned to them. All these attributes and many more are in the domain of a shaman, who is an explorer of worlds and a practitioner of knowledge gained. Let us now explore the magical world of the plant kingdom.

Alphabetical List of Herbs

Acacia	Mammillaria cacti
Agara	Mescal Bean
Anadenanthera	Mexican Buckeye
Ashvaganda	Mexican Poppy
Astrophytum	Morning Glory
Ayahuasca	Mushroom Madness
Bakana	Nutmeg
Betel Nut	Ololiuqui
Blue Water Lily	Orchids
Brugmansia	Pancratium
Calea	Peyote
Canavalia	Peyote Cimarrón
Chacruna	Peyotillo
Chaliponga	Piule
Cawe	Puffballs
Coca	Saguaro
Coleus	Salvia divinorum
Copelandia	Scirpus
Damiana	Screw Pine
Dita	Senecio
Dolichothele	Sida
Esakuna	Sinicuichi
Hawaiian Baby Woodrose	Solandra
Hikuli Mulato	Tagetes
Hikuri	Teonacatl
Homalomena	Toloache
Iboga	Torna Loca
Justicia	Vanilla Cactus
Kava Kava	Voacanga
Khat	Yohimbe
Maguey	

A

Acacia
Fabaceae
Other common names: Wattle

The genus acacia is made up of hundreds of species of tree, mainly from Australia, but now distributed in many parts of the world. These trees are often grown for their ornamental appeal with their finely divided foliage and attractive flowers, but the trees have many other uses. The acacias are included here because DMT (Dimethyltryptamine) and other psychoactive alkaloids have been isolated from the bark. *Acacia maidenii* is one of the species that has been used, and *A. simplex* is another.

There is much debate about the authenticity of claims about psychoactive substances contained in acacias and the aboriginal people of Australia do not use the trees for these purposes. However, this has not stopped neo-shamans of the modern world being very interested in these trees and from experimenting with extracts taken from them. Acacia bark has been used as a DMT-containing herbal ingredient in ayahuasca mixtures (see the description of ayahuasca later in this work).

Acacias can generally be legally grown and so the seeds of various species are readily available.

Agara
Galbulimima belgraveana
Himantandraceae
Other common names: Kombe

The agara is a large tree growing to 90ft. in height and found growing in Malaysia, Papua New Guinea, Molucca and Northeast Australia. The flowers are yellow or a brownish-yellow and are composed of stamens only, having no petals or sepals. The agara bears red fleshy fruit, which smells of resin. The leaves are a

5

metallic shade of green above and quite glossy in appearance, while the undersides are brownish. They are elliptic in shape and reach about 6in. in length. The tree has a greyish brown bark that has a strong aroma.

Natives of Papua are reported to make an intoxicating tea from the leaves and bark by boiling them with the leaves of the plant called ereiba (*Homalomena lauterbachii*) and to employ this for a pre-battle hallucinogenic experience. Psilocybin-containing mushrooms may also be consumed with this mixture. This shamanic brew is said to produce a state of intoxication in which visions of men and animals are seen and followed by a deep slumber. However, there are no records of Australian Aborigines using the tree in this way.

According to Schultes and Hofmann in their classic work *Plants of the Gods*, although some 28 separate alkaloids have been isolated from the tree, none of these have been demonstrated to be psychoactive. Included amongst these alkaloids are himandrine, himbacine, himgravine, himbosine and himbadine.

Anadenanthera
Anadenanthera colubrina, A. peregrina
Fabaceae
Other common names: Vilca, Cebil, Yopo, Cohoba

Anadenanthera is a genus of tropical trees from South America with seeds, pods and bark that contain DMT, bufotenin and other short-acting tryptamines. The seeds are ground up to produce a hallucinogenic snuff which shamans of indigenous tribes of Colombia, Venezuela and the Brazilian rainforest area use to experience visions and in healing ceremonies and rituals. Yopo snuff was also commonly used in the Caribbean islands, where the trees also grow, up until the time of the Spanish Conquest.

The snuff is often administered by having another person blow it into the nostrils using a bamboo tube, or it can be snorted up bird-bone tubes. Archaeological research has shown that these trees were used as hallucinogenic snuffs 4,000 years ago. Puma bone smoking pipes have been found along with anadenanthera beans at Inca Cueva in Argentina, and snuff trays and tubes were discovered in the central Peruvian coast dating back to 1200 BCE.

Anadenanthera tree bark and seeds have also been used by various tribes in ayahuasca mixtures where it is combined with the caapi vine to increase the potency.

Ashvaganda
Withania somnifera
Solanaceae
Other common names: Kuthmithi

This plant from the very large nightshade family is a semi-hardy shrub found growing in parts of Africa and India.

In Indian Ayurvedic medicine it is used as a tranquiliser and narcotic. Its sedative properties are suggested by its botanical species name *somnifera*, meaning 'bringing sleep'. The roots of ashvaganda are used for this purpose in Africa. It is also employed as a health-giving tonic and as an aphrodisiac, and these are qualities said to be provided by the closely related orobal (A. aristata), a medicinal shrub found in Tenerife and some of the other Canary Islands where it is regarded as a most important herbal medicine and all-round panacea. The whole ashvaganda plant has medicinal and psychoactive properties and it can be used to make a pain-killing tea.

Ashvaganda is an easy plant to cultivate, and once established, after a period of winter dormancy, will regrow itself quickly from the rootstock.

Astrophytum
Astrophytum asterias, Astrophytum capricorne, Astrophytum myriostigma
Cactaceae
Other common names: Peyotillo, Bishop's Cap

The *Astrophytum* cacti, which are to be found in Mexico, bear a superficial resemblance to peyote, and have been reported as regarded as peyote substitutes by the Tarahumara tribe. The name 'bishop's cap' is mainly used for the species *myriostigma* and indicates the shape and appearance of the cactus. These unusual and attractive desert plants are popular with cactus-collectors, as well as being sought after by would-be 'peyotists' and have become very rare in their wild habitats. Due to the ongoing threats to their survival, the *Astrophytum* cacti are protected by conservation laws. Although various potentially psychoactive alkaloids have been identified, the amounts are very small and the stronger hallucinogenic substances mescaline and macromerine have not been found in these plants.

Ayahuasca
Banisteriopsis caapi
Malpighiaceae
Other common names: Caapi, Yagé, Vine of the Soul

Ayahuasca Vine (Photo: Iolo Jones)

No book about the use of sacred herbs by shamans of the south would be complete without including the psychoactive and healing brew known as ayahuasca, which is also known as iowaska, or yagé. There are books and other publications about ayahuasca, and its use has even caused religious movements, such as Santo Daime, to come about that use it as a sacred healing ritual. The word ayahuasca actually means 'vine of the soul' and refers to a beverage made by brewing bark-covered sections of the caapi vine along with other herbal ingredients.

Ayahuasca has a long history of use by shamans of tribes from the Amazon rainforest areas. It contains beta-carboline alkaloids harmine, harmaline and tetrahydroharmine which are monoamine oxidase inhibitors (MAOIs). MAOIs should not be consumed along with any foods containing tryptophans, as well as sauerkraut, coffee, cocoa, chocolate, cheese, dairy produce, avocados, bananas, figs, pineapples, broad beans, pickled herring, chicken liver, nutmeg, liquorice and yeast extract. Antihistamines, amphetamines, sedatives, tranquilisers and narcotics should all be avoided too, along with the drugs ecstasy, macromerine, mescaline, ephedrine and the essential oils of fennel, dill and parsley. This is because a MAOI in the presence of any of the foods, ingredients and drugs on that long list can produce a potentially dangerous condition in which headaches, vomiting, blood pressure crises and heart failure can occur. Ideally, several days before and after consumption of an MAOI or ayahuasca should be observed before any of those foods or substances are consumed. This is why tribal shamans often stick to strict diet restrictions before the use of the brew. However, there are ayahuasca groups that do not adhere to dieting restrictions which suggests that dangerous situations regarding the health of the consumer are not encountered often. It is still better to be safe than sorry though!

The reason that ayahuasca is such a well-respected psycho-active drink is because the exceedingly potent hallucinogenic substance DMT (dimethyltryptamine) becomes active in anyone who has consumed it along with the MAOIs supplied by the vine. Otherwise DMT only works if snorted as snuff and is of much shorter duration. The ayahuasca brew is a mixture of the caapi vine and other plants which contain DMT. The main ones of these are chacruna (*Psychotria viridis*) and chaliponga (*Dilopterys cabrerana*).

The ayahuasca experience is very intense and often includes a period of vomiting but this is regarded as beneficial as a purge. Extreme hallucinatory states ensue and there may well be voices heard and encounters with beings viewed as spirit guides and other-dimensional entities. Healings of physical and mental conditions may occur and the ayahuasca user may have life-changing realisations. Shamans and experienced ayahuasca users recommend that you do not take this brew on your own.

Author and conspiracy theorist David Icke used his ayahuasca sessions as the inspiration for his book *Tales from the Time Loop*.

The laws covering ayahuasca vary from country to country and are subject to change. DMT is a controlled substance in the UK, US and elsewhere but plants containing it are often legal to possess.

B

Bakana
Coryphantha compacta
Cactaceae
Other common names: Beehive Cactus, Bakanawa, Hikuli,
Wichuri

The cactus known as bakana is found in dry, hilly locations,
and is difficult to spot as it nestles concealed and camouflaged
against the sandy soil. To avoid confusion, it is worth noting
that the name 'bakana' is also used by the Tarahumara Indians
of Mexico for a totally unrelated but equally psychoactive plant
– the sedge *Scirpus atrovirens* (covered later on in this book). The
Tarahumara consider bakana, a small, round and spiny cactus,
as a variety of peyote (covered in depth in a later section), and
this is not surprising because this species and many other cacti in
this genus have been found to contain a variety of psychoactive
phenethylamines.

The alkaloid macromerine, which is similar to mescaline but
weaker in action in proportion to the amount needed, is derived
from its well-known cousin the Donana cactus (*C. macromeris*)
from the northern part of Mexico. The species *compacta* is greatly
feared and respected by Indian shamans from the areas in which
it is found, and its close relative *C. palmerii* is also used as an
entheogen in Mexico.

Betel Nut
Areca catechu
Palmaceae
Other common names: Areca Palm, Areca Nuts, Guvka, Pinang,
Pinlang

There exists a lot of confusion with the plant substance known
as 'betel nut' because the 'nut' that is chewed by millions of

11

Betel Nuts (Photo: Iolo Jones)

people is actually a combination of the seed of the areca palm mixed with lime and wrapped in a leaf from the betel pepper (*Piper betel*). The areca palm tree bears yellowish-red fruit the size of hens' eggs, which contain the brown acorn-sized seeds or 'nuts' and these are mottled inside like nutmegs. These seeds are cut into pieces before being rolled in lime and wrapped in the leaves of the betel pepper. The betel nuts are then generally held in the mouth rather than actually chewed, although the terms 'chewing betel nuts' and 'betel chewing' are commonly employed to describe this very widespread practice. It is estimated that as many as between one quarter and one tenth of the world's population indulge in this habit which is practised from East Africa to Polynesia, including India as a stronghold of the practice. In fact, shiploads of the seeds are exported annually from Sumatra, Molucca, China and Siam.

Betel nuts are so popular because of the stimulant and intoxicating properties of the alkaloids arecaine (also known as arecaidine) and arecoline, which are released as a result of a chemical reaction engendered by the alkaline lime in the mixture. The people of these countries chew betel nuts all day long, and regular partakers of this custom have stained teeth and mouths because the seeds release a strong red dye into the saliva. The taste is actually very acid and astringent, which causes users to spit it out as they continue chewing but it is also aromatic. In India and other parts of the world, perfumes and other additives are often added to the broken up seeds to further improve the mixture, and this product is known as supari. It is readily available from Asian grocers and food-stores.

The betel nut also contains large amounts of tannin, giving it astringent properties, as well as another alkaloid known as guracine together with gallic acid, fixed oil gum, volatile oil, lignin and various saline substances. Arecoline hydrobromide, a commercial salt related to one of the main alkaloids, is a strong stimulant with laxative properties. In veterinary practice it is used to treat colic in horses. The betel nut has been made into a dentifrice because of its astringent qualities. In India it has been employed as a means of removing tapeworms from the body.

In a much more shamanic way, the sweet-scented flowers of the tree are used in Borneo as medicinal charms to aid the healing of the sick. The betel nuts are also made into magical amulets to ward off evil. It is believed in parts of India that the deities in the heavenly worlds lack betel there, so this makes it an excellent offering to the gods.

The betel pepper grows in the same countries and is cultivated on trellises as a climbing shrub, with the leaves being harvested and dried. The plant contains cadinene, betel-phenol, chavicol, and a volatile oil, which is yellow when it is a good quality. The leaves have similar properties to the 'nut' being a stimulant, an aromatic and an astringent bitter. They also have antiseptic qualities and the oil from them is used against respiratory complaints in the form of a gargle and as an inhalant.

Blue Water Lily
Nymphaea caerulea, N.ampla
Nymphaceae
Other common names: Blue Lotus, Egyptian Lotus, Sacred Narcotic Lily of the Nile

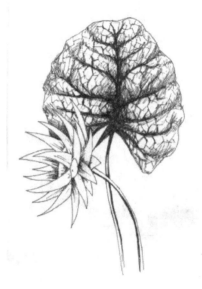

Blue Water Lily (Illustration: Aziz Ipsule)

The blue water lily is a truly beautiful flower and just looking at it in awe and wonder it would be very easy to think it had magical qualities, and from what we can tell it does in a chemically-driven mind-altering way. It is believed by many people to have been used as an entheogenic herb for shamanic purposes, and also perhaps for recreation, by the ancient Egyptians. This is because the plant's leaves and flower-heads are often conspicuous in artwork that survives from the period of the mighty empires of the pharaohs. It was even discovered in an excavation in 1922, that the blue lotus lily had been scattered over the mummified body of Tutankhamun when he had been laid to rest in his tomb.

Other scholars have argued against its entheogenic usage,

possibly in an effort to hold the Egyptian culture somewhat above the world of drug-users. The viewpoint that this water lily was used for its psychoactive properties was, however, demonstrated to be very likely, when in a British Channel 4 television series called *The Sacred Weeds*, a couple of volunteers ingested the plant and became clearly intoxicated. In fact, they enjoyed the experience so much they were allowed back for a second portion. An expert non-believer and sceptic was clearly challenged by this demonstration and had to concur that it looked as if the blue water lily might be psychoactive after all.

The herb contains apomorphine, nuciferine, and nornuciferine as alkaloids that have been extracted from the rhizome, and these substances are thought to be responsible for its psychotropic activity in humans who ingest it.

Besides growing in Egypt and in the area of the Nile, this water lily is also found in Tanzania and Kenya, as well as being cultivated around the world for its very great ornamental qualities.

Similarly, the Mexican water lily with the botanical name of *N. ampla,* has been linked with shamanic usage by the American Indian tribes of the Central part of the continent, and is again depicted in architecture and artwork. It has been reported to have been used in recent times as a recreational drug-plant with narcotic and hallucinogenic properties. This water lily is very similar in appearance and growing habits, found in lakes, slow-moving rivers and in large ponds, but the flower is white. It is also found growing in other temperate and tropical zones of both hemispheres of the planet.

It is perhaps significant that the ancient empires on both sides of the ocean appeared to employ the water lily as a sacred shamanic herb in their ceremonies and artwork. Several authors have commented on other similarities such as the pyramid-style buildings once made, as well as many similar etymological roots and derivations in the languages and dialects. The probable use of the blue water lily as a sacred narcotic herb by cultures of the Old and New Worlds certainly points the argument in favour of a belief in a common ancestry or origin. The water lilies are governed by the Moon in herbal and astrological lore.

Brugmansia

Brugmansia arborea, B. aurea, B. insignis, B. sanguinea, B. suaveolens, B. versicolor, B. vulcanicola

Solanaceae

Other common names: Angel's Trumpet, Angel's Tears

The *Brugmansia* species grow as large bushes and small trees. They come from South America, from Colombia, Chile, Brazil, Ecuador and Venezuela, though all seven named species are now thought to be probably extinct in the wild. However, because of their very great beauty and ornamental value, the *Brugmansias* are often grown in gardens and parks in subtropical and tropical areas of the world.

They have large trumpet-shaped flowers that hang down in bunches and come in a range of white, pink, yellow, orange and red shades, according to species or variety. There are many cultivars and hybrids, and the plants are usually propagated by cuttings. The flowers are pollinated by hawkmoths and emit a strong perfume, especially at night. The red-flowered *B. sanguinea* emits no scent, however, and it is pollinated by hummingbirds.

The *Brugmansia* genus is closely related to the very similar *Datura* genus of plants, and *Brugmansias* used to be called 'tree daturas'. The *Brugmansia* species tend to grow a lot taller than the *Daturas* and they have pendulous flowers that are followed by smooth-skinned seedpods. The *Daturas* have upright flowers and their seedpods are usually protected with spines, hence the name 'thorn-apple', which is applied to the species *D. stramonium*. *Brugmansia* and *Datura* species all contain the tropane alkaloids scopolamine, hyoscyamine and atropine, making them very dangerous poisonous plants. The alkaloids are concentrated in the leaves and seeds but all parts are toxic to humans. Scopolamine has been used by criminals as an aid to robbery by rendering their victims unconscious or controllable. It has been linked too with cases of rape, and has acquired a very 'bad' name as a drug.

Hallucinations are part of the intoxication brought on by *Brugmansia* poisoning and so the plants have been used by shamans as entheogens in religious ceremonies and rituals, however, the consumption of these herbs puts the user in very great danger. The poisons in a *Brugmansia* can cause insanity, long-term physical and mental harm and death. Nevertheless, dangerous as they can be, the *Brugmansias* are sometimes added as ingredients used to make ayahuasca brews.

C

Calea
Calea zachatechichi
Asteraceae
Other common names: Dream Herb, Leaf of God

The Dream herb has fast become a plant of increasing interest in ethnobotanical circles of enquiry, and not surprisingly, for this herb has a long history of shamanic use by various Mexican tribes. Besides this, the plant exhibits some effects quite unlike those of many herbs of this nature, the chief of these being its ability to induce dreaming and recollection of these reveries. This effect due to the consumption of this herb has been called 'oneirogenic', meaning dream-inducing.

The Calea herb was reported in 1968, by naturalist Thomas MacDougall, as a 'secret plant' used by the Chontal Indians of Mexico, amongst whom he was working at the time. It was said that these people would find somewhere they could be alone and undisturbed and then drink a tea of the herb, combining this with the smoking of a cigarette of the dried leaves. This practice led to drowsiness and a sort of clairvoyant trance state or sleep in which 'visions seen in dreams' were experienced. A good feeling of relaxation and well-being apparently stayed with the user for a day or so afterwards. Furthermore, MacDougall informs us that the Indians know when they have taken a sufficient dose because they will feel drowsy and also become aware of the heart beating and their pulse rate.

The shamans of the Chontal tribe state that the herb is able to 'clarify the senses', and say that they use it for divinatory messages. For example, if a lost person or object needs to be found, then the herb would be consulted by the shaman seeking a solution to the mystery, and the answer to the hidden location will be seen in a dream. Schultes and Hofmann tell us that it is these people who refer to the Calea plant as 'Leaf of God' or

'Thle-pelakano'.

Scientific researchers have backed up these astonishing claims by a series of tests on volunteers. Healthy human guinea pigs for the experiment were administered low doses of extracts from the plant against a double-blind test where the other volunteers were given a placebo. After the experiment those who had taken the herbal extracts scored much higher with regard to reaction time and their estimation of time-lapse. Not only that but in another trial examining the effects of a controlled nap taken by the same group of twelve volunteers, it was discovered that the beginning stages of sleep were induced earlier on in those who had been given the dream herb. As well as this, there were more spontaneous awakenings by those in this group. Furthermore again, subjective reports on the dreams of the test group were higher amongst those who had taken the extract than by those on a placebo or who had been given the tranquilizer Valium. Researchers felt that this showed a measurable increase in hypnagogic imagery in the early stages of sleep.

From the above, it can be seen that Calea is a herb that justifies a lot more research with regard to its unique neuropharmacological properties. But it is not only used in this way for it is traditionally also used medicinally as a poultice for skin complaints as well as for treating fevers, gastric problems and mild diarrhoea. It has been valued as an insecticide too. The herb appears to owe some of its effects to a repulsive mixture of 'bitters', which are correctly identified as sesquiterpenelactones, and its Mexican and species name 'zacatechichi' means 'bitter grass'. Calea also contains an unidentified psychoactive alkaloid and flavones.

The dream herb can be found growing wild from Mexico to Costa Rica and seems to prefer rich soils, plenty of water and sunlight, although it is a hardy perennial and quite drought and frost resistant. It can grow quite tall reaching as much as 9ft. and bears woody branches and stems with small oval serrated leaves. The flowers are small and a shade of yellow or white.

Calea can be propagated by seed or cuttings, although the seeds are notoriously difficult to germinate and the latter method is far more common. The usual dose of the dried leaves is about 2 tablespoons or a small handful of dried leaves to a pint of water. The tea is made by brewing the leaves for 5 minutes in boiled water and then straining. The cups of the resulting liquid are to be sipped and followed by a few tokes on a cigarette of the dried leaves. As yet, no harmful side effects have been reported but this in no way means that it has the all-clear, and it is likely that many people would find the awareness of their pulse rate quite alarming.

Finally in this description of the dream herb, here is a very detailed account of an alternative method of consumption, permission for republication kindly allowed by Torsten of the Shaman Australis Ethnobotanicals website.

I was introduced to this herb in the early '90s in the form of an alcoholic extract. My favourite method of ingesting was to get myself prepared for bed in the evening, and then put 15 drops under my tongue. Sitting mellow and comfortable, a slight wave of tiredness would come over me about 10 minutes later, lasting only a couple of minutes. If this wave was ignored, there would be no further effect, but if I went to bed straight away, I would drift off to sleep within a few minutes, 'hypnotised' by my slow but very amplified heartbeat. I would have many dreams of a profound and insightly nature (at least that's how it felt at the time), which I would remember in detail in the morning. There was a slight euphoric feeling that went with the realisation of these dreams, or maybe it was just a really good night's sleep, but the mornings always had an upbeat note to them (in spite of the fact I generally dislike mornings). If I was awoken within the first hour of going to sleep, I would be surprised by the number and profoundness of my dreams in such a short timespan, but would not have any more of this type of dreams after falling asleep again. Sadly the extract from the same supplier no longer has that effect on me, and no other supplier ever produced an extract that could elicit these effects. This is why I started making my own from my homegrown herb. It is not done by Soxthlet extraction, which I believe destroys many active components, including that of Calea zacatechichi, and my method involves no heat applied to the material at any point in the manufacture, yet it is concentrated to reduce the amount of alcohol and the 'volume of bitterness'.

Canavalia
Canavalia maritima
Fabaceae
Other common names: Frijol de Playa

The herb *Canavalia maritima* is, as its species name suggests, a plant of the coastal areas, growing wild in Mexico but also in the tropical and semi-tropical parts of North and South America, as well as in Africa. It is a spreading prostrate shrub with woody stems reaching as much as 30ft. in length and bearing large thick leaflets in groups of 3, as well as pink showy flowers, similar to those of beans, in flowering spikes followed by brown pods. These pods can be as much as 4in. in length and 1in. wide.

The plant is included in this work because it has been reported to have been used as a marijuana substitute when smoked by people who have found it growing along the Gulf Coast of Mexico. Also, seeds of the shrub have been discovered in graves in Oaxaca and Yucatan, Mexico, as well as in others in Peru, with these burial sites dating from 3000 BCE to 900 CE. Although, no other evidence has been forthcoming, it seems possible that this plant was once used for shamanic purposes and in rituals. The alkaloid L-betonicine has been isolated from the plant but has not tested positive as a hallucinogen or intoxicant in research so far.

Chacruna
Psychotria viridis
Rubiaceae
Other common names: Chacrona

Chacruna is the name given to a perennial shrub found in South America, and which is used as a very important ingredient of ayahuasca brews. Chacruna, which can grow to as much as 16ft. in height, is an excellent source of DMT.

The plant is usually propagated by cuttings and these cuttings are often just leaves taken from the plant. Even a section of a leaf lightly pushed into compost will root. Chacruna is grown this way because it has a very low rate of germination. Growing Chacruna is legal in many parts of the world but the drug DMT it contains is not. In fact, DMT is classified as a Schedule 1 drug under the United Nations 1971 Convention on Psychotropic Substances.

Chaliponga
Diplopterys cabrerana
Malpighiaceae
Other common names: Chagropanga, Chacruna (in Ecuador)

Chaliponga is a South American vine found in Brazil, Colombia, Ecuador and Peru, and in parts of Ecuador, it is often called Chacruna, which is confusing because this name is also used for *Psychotria viridis*. It is easy to see where this confusion arose, however, because both plants are used as main admixture herbs added as ingredients for the making of ayahuasca. This is because it contains DMT, 5-MeO-DMT and bufotenin, substances that become activated as hallucinogens when in the presence of the beta-carboline alkaloids in the caapi vine bark. Like chacrona, this plant is usually propagated in the form of cuttings.

C

Cawe
Pachycereus pecten-aboriginum
Cactaceae
Other common names: Wichowaka

Cawe is the Tarahumara Indian name for a tall cactus species, which grows in Mexico and reaches about 35ft. in height. It has short grey spines all over it and bears purplish flowers with white inner parts. These grow to about 3in. across. Cawe is also known by these Tarahumara people as 'Wichowaka', which translated from their language means insanity.

This cactus species has several uses, being used for various medical problems, as well as being a shamanic inebriant. The Indians prepare a drink from the juice of the young branches and this is reported to cause both giddiness and hallucinations, probably due to the 4-hydroxy-3-methoxyphenylethylamine it contains along with four tetrahydroisoquinoline alkaloids. Cawe is also reported to contain mescaline, and has been sold by some suppliers of ethnobotanicals as a cactus species that is a source of this very psychoactive substance.

Coca
Erythroxylum coca
Erythroxylaceae

Coca is a shrub or small tree that is the source of the highly addictive stimulant drug known as cocaine, which is illegal and has caused addiction problems worldwide. However, the leaves of coca, when chewed, also for their stimulating effects, have been a traditional part of the culture of tribal people of Colombia, Peru, Ecuador, Chile, Northern Argentina and Bolivia for thousands of years. Mummies, dating back 3,000 years, have been found with traces of coca. The shamans in these countries where the plant is grown use coca leaves and have done since pre-Inca and pre-Columbian times. The coca leaf chewing helps provide energy for long periods of prayer and meditation. It is done in the form of a quid, which is made from a few leaves and can be held in the mouth against the gums. Some forms of alkaline substance, such as lime, bicarbonate of soda, or quinoa ashes, are traditionally used too to activate the properties of the leaves. Coca leaves can also be made into a tea, known as 'mate de coca'. Consumption of it is of known benefit to the health of the consumer, because coca is a good source of the minerals calcium, phosphorus and potassium, as well as being rich in vitamins B1, B2, C and E.

The Kogi, Arhuaco and Wiwa tribes of the Sierra Nevada de Santa Marta mountain in Colombia all use coca, and the men use a device known as a poporo to aid their consumption of the herb in a traditional and sacred way. Lime is transferred from the poporo to the leaves being chewed with the aid of a stick. This is done because, as already explained, the lime is alkaline and serves to activate the stimulant properties of the leaves. The poporo is made from a gourd and symbolises the womb, while the stick is an obvious phallic symbol. When a young man is ready to marry he is instructed in the use of coca and the poporo, which is a mark of manhood. In the Kogi, this initiation is supervised by a 'mamo/mama', which is the name given to the shamanic leaders of the tribe, who are selected for this rank by a process of divination.

The coca plant has two species, which have two varieties each. They are *Erythroxylum coca* var. *coca, E. coca var. ipadu, E. novogranatense var. novogranatense and E. novogranatense var. truxillense*. Coca is often cultivated as a cash crop, despite the illegal status of its leaves and the drug cocaine in many parts of the world. There is even a new form of the plant, known as 'supercoca', that is resistant to the glyphosate herbicide. The origins of this new strain are debatable, and in Colombia, the government, with the aid of American financial and military backing, have had an eradication programme.

Coleus

Coleus blumei (**Syn.** *C.x hybridus* **vars**), *C. pumila*
Lamiaceae
Other common names: Flame Nettle, Painted Nettle

Coleus (Photo: Iolo Jones)

The coleus is an incredibly striking and ornamental plant from the sage and mint family, and with its bold colours of purple, maroon, various shades of red and pink, yellow, gold, white and green, and in many variations of leaf-forms, it certainly looks like it should have psychedelic effects. It also bears small spikes of bluish-purple flowers but these are very insignificant against its otherwise very showy display of colour. The coleus plant is grown worldwide as a houseplant and is very popular and well-known for rather obvious reasons. What is not quite so well known is that it is reputed to be capable of producing an intoxication with hallucinations and visual patterns said to be similar to those produced by psilocybin mushrooms, and that it can even cause telepathic insights. The effect of the coleus has also been likened to that of its definitely psychoactive cousin the diviner's mint (*Salvia divinorum*) and the possibly psychoactive scarlet sage (*S. splendens*), both of which are covered later on in this book.

It is reported that the coleus, although native to the Philippines, was recognised and adopted by the Mazatec Indian shamans from Mexico, as a divinatory herb. Also it has been suggested that these Indians may turn to this plant when magic mushroom supplies are low, however, the truth of these matters is debatable. The story goes that the coleus is known by various names in Mexico to denote its variety and characteristics. One species of coleus (*C. pumila*) is referred to as 'El Macho' (The Male), while another type is known as 'La Hembra' (The Female), and this is supposedly related to the diviner's mint. Two types of *C. blumei* are identified as 'El Nene' (The Child) and the other as 'El Ahijado' (The Godson). Many experts on botany and horticulture, however, would argue that the so-called *C. blumei* is actually a hybrid of several species and should be correctly called *Coleus* x hybridus vars.

As to the means of taking this plant, about 50 to 70 large fresh leaves are chewed very thoroughly and swallowed to produce an intoxicated and hallucinatory state. It is also reported that the leaves can be steeped in lukewarm water for an hour, strained, and then the liquid is drunk. Gareth Rose, in *The Psychedelics*, states that the leaves can also be smoked, although how you go about smoking fresh leaves he fails to explain. This author goes on to point out that although no harmful effects are known of, some people do experience some nausea but this fades away, and the resulting 'trip' lasts around two hours.

Coleus is very bitter and unpleasant to the taste when eaten fresh and in such large quantities, so it is hardly surprising some people get nauseous, but apart from the displeasure experienced while eating the leaves, many contemporary neo-shamans (myself included) have reported a lack of success with it as an intoxicant or hallucinogen. Other people, however, have reported that it does work. The truth, as they say is out there, but with this fascinating plant the debate continues. Whatever the truth may be, it is certainly a most attractive greenhouse or indoor plant, or for the garden in warmer climates.

Copelandia
Copelandia cyanescens (Syn. *Paneolus cyanescens*)
Coprinaceae
Other common names: Blue Meanies

Copelandia cyanescens is a fungus found in many tropical and subtropical areas of the globe but is well known from being cultivated in Bali where it gets sold to hippies and tourists in search of an exotic and powerful natural high. The *Copelandia* mushroom is also used by the Indonesian islanders to help celebrate their festivals, and it is grown on cattle and buffalo dung for this purpose.

It is a small greyish-brown mushroom of fleshy appearance and with a campanulate cap born on a slender and fragile stem, which reaches just over 4in. in height. Like its species and nickname suggests, this fungus stains blue when bruised, which is a traditional visual test for the presence of the strong psychoactive tryptamines psilocybin and psilocin. In fact, it is thought to have one of the strongest concentrations of these substances in its flesh with amounts as high as up to 1.2% of psilocin and 0.6% of psilocybin.

Although it is mainly found growing in the tropics and semi-tropics, including Queensland and New South Wales in Australia amongst locations it has been found in, a batch of these mushrooms was once found in a garden in France. It is from these mushrooms that the initial discovery that *Copelandia* was a psilocybin-containing species was made.

This species of psychoactive mushroom, whilst having similarities in its hallucinogenic active constituents and in its botanical and common names both giving a clue to its colouration when bruised, is not to be confused with *Psilocybe cyanescens*. This magic mushroom is commonly known as 'blue saucers' or 'wavy caps', and is often found in great numbers in late autumn growing in clusters in shrub borders and other places where wood-chip mulch has been spread. It occurs in North America, Europe, and lately, probably carried in mulch, in the UK as well.

D

Damiana
Turnera diffusa (Syn. *T. aphrodisiaca*)
Turneraceae

Damiana is described in depth in my book on *Herbs of the Northern Shaman*, but deserves to be included again here too because Mexico is one of the main countries in which it is found. It also grows wild in Texas, South America and parts of the West Indies.

The herb is actually a small and aromatic shrub, which bears pale green ovo-lanceolate leaves and small yellow flowers arising from the axils of the leaves. It is bitter to taste and contains a greenish volatile oil smelling a bit like chamomile (*Anthemis nobilis*), resins, tannin, and a bitter principle known as damianin. The action of damiana is as a mild purgative, tonic and diuretic. Damiana is also famous as an aphrodisiac and does appear to have a stimulant and tonic effect on the sexual organs.

The reason it is included in this book, however, is because many people find that it can be used as a legal marijuana substitute, by either smoking the herb or drinking it as a tea. Some people like to do both. The dried leaves are the parts that are used. Damiana is readily available from herbal and ethnobotanical suppliers.

Dita
Alstonia scholaris
Apocynaceae
Other common names: Australian Fever Bush, Bitter Bark, Devil's Bit, Devil Tree, Pali-mara, White Cheesewood

The dita is an evergreen tree that grows between 50 and 80ft. tall and is found in India, Molucca, the Philippines, and parts of northeast tropical Australia. The genus *Alstonia* takes its name from the once Professor of Botany in Edinburgh. It has a furrowed and spongy bark, which contains a very bitter sap. The leaves are oblong in shape and long and glossy in appearance, whilst the flowers are greenish-white, tubular in formation and carried in dense clusters in the spring. The flowers are followed by long cylindrical fruits. The tree likes a rich soil and an open and sunny location. It is sensitive to drought and frost-tender.

Medicinally it is used in India to treat such diverse ailments as malaria, skin diseases, asthma, and epilepsy, as well as diarrhoea, for disorders of the bowel and as an antithelmintic. In Australia, some Aborigine tribes use the sticky latex sap as an adhesive to glue feathers and other adornments to their bodies. Possibly this has some psychoactive effect by absorption through the skin but this is only conjecture. However, it is known that back in India, followers of Tantric sex-cults and sects use the seeds of this species and the closely related *Alstonia venenata* for their stimulant and aphrodisiac properties.

The seeds of the dita tree are rich in the potentially hallucinogenic indole alkaloids alstovenine, chlorogenine, ditamine, echitamine, reserpine and venenatine together with chlorogenic acid. This last-mentioned acid is a known mild irritant to the bladder and urethra, which increases sensitivity to the genitals and urinary tract. The alkaloids ditamine, echitamine and echtenine are present in the latex and bark.

Dolichothele
Dolichothele baumii, D. longimamma, D. melalenca, D. sphaerica, D. surculosa, D. uberiformis
Cactaceae

The Mexican Dolichothele cacti have been reported as being used for shamanic purposes by various tribes. The cacti are regarded as substitute peyote and research has identified small amounts of potentially psychoactive alkaloids, including N-methylphenethylamine, B-O-methylsynephrine, N-methyltyramine, synephrine, hordenine, and dolicotheline (N-isovalerylhistamine).

E

Esakuna
Cymbopogon densiflorus
Graminaceae

The perennial grass known as esakuna grows wild in Gabon, the Congo and Nyasaland, and bears brownish-green flowering spikes and typical grass-like leaves. These leaves and the underground rhizome have a pleasant citrus smell and the plant and others in its genus are rich in essential oils.

In Tanganyika, the tribal shamans are known to smoke the flowering tops on their own, or mixed in with tobacco, with the purpose of causing prophetic dreams and visions.

Steroidal substances have been found in some species of the genus and the leaves and rhizomes are used as a tonic and styptic by the people of the areas in which the herb grows. However, the compounds responsible for any hallucinogenic or narcotic effects are unknown.

H

Hawaiian Baby Woodrose
Argyreia nervosa
Convolvulaceae
Other common names: Elephant Creeper, Woolly Morning Glory

The Hawaiian baby woodrose is a most attractive vine from the same family as the morning glory (*Ipomoea*), and, like its cousin, this climber also contains lysergic acid amides, which make it a strong hallucinogen and herb of divinatory and potential recreational usage. Unlike the morning glory, however, which comes from Central America, this plant's place of origin is in India. It has been taken to many other countries as an ornamental plant, and in the islands of Polynesia and Hawaii, it has found favour with the local shamans of the Kahunas who have used it as a divination sacrament. It has also been used as a recreational drug because its effects can be similar to LSD.

There are a few unpleasant side effects, however, such as nausea, and this is probably due to the varying amounts of alkaloids in the seeds and the strychnine in the fuzzy seed coatings. It is advisable to scrape this layer off before ingesting and no more than a maximum of 7 of the large seeds should be taken at the same time. A starting dose is 3 or 4 and it is important to remember that the seeds need to be chewed very well for the lysergic acid amides to be ingested. The 'trip' can last some 4–6 hours or even longer, and this needs to be taken into account.

The vine has large heart-shaped leaves, covered in a whitish down on the undersides. The flowers are quite large too and very beautiful to look at, borne as they are on pendulous stalks. Their funnel-shapes are a light purplish colour with a much deeper shade of the same colour in the throats. These flowers are followed by pods containing 4 seeds.

Hikuli Mulato
Epithelantha micromeris
Cactaceae
Other common names: Hikuli Rosapara, Button Cactus, Pingpong Ball Cactus

'Hikuli mulato', as this small globular cactus is known to the Indians, grows in Mexico and some of the southern states of North America. It is covered in spines, giving it a greyish appearance, and is one of the 'false peyotes' of the Tarahumara and Huichol Indians of Chihuahua in Mexico. The cactus is also referred to as the 'dark-skinned peyotl', though this must have a symbolic meaning because the spines of the cactus make it look anything but 'dark'. Shamans of the tribe claim that they ingest this cactus to make their sight clearer and also to communicate in a magical way with fellow sorcerers. Tarhumara runners use it as a stimulant and a 'protector'. They also regard the cactus as able to prolong life expectancy. Another belief holds that it has the power to make evil people insane and to send them to their destruction by falling over cliffs. The older plants, which form clusters, are the ones that are reported to have these magical powers. These specimens have been given the name 'rospara'.

This button cactus species has small pink flowers arising from the wool at the centre of the plant and these are followed by bright red edible fruit called 'chilitos'. Hikuli mulato cactus contains at least 6 triterpenes and various other alkaloids, including tyramine and hordenine which may account for its properties. The cacti have their spines removed before consumption and both fresh and dried cacti are said to be psychoactive.

H

Hikuri
Echinocereus triglochidiatus, E. salmdyckianus
Cactaceae
Other common names: Pitallito

Two cacti commonly known as 'hikuri' or 'pitallito' are both of the genus *Echinocereus*, and both are regarded as 'false peyotes' by the Tarahumaras of Mexico. Both cacti grow in the mountainous areas and are quite similar apart from the fact that the species *E. salmdyckianus* has orange flowers about 3–4in. long, and the other species has smaller scarlet flowers that reach 2–3in. only. The former type has yellowish-green stems and 7–9 ribs bearing 8 or 9 yellow radial spines, while the latter cactus has a deep-green stem and fewer radial spines which turn grey as they mature. The cacti form cylindrical mounds up to 2ft. in height and are quite resistant to both cold and drought.

It is said that the Indians regard these cacti as having 'high mental qualities' and that they sing to them as they harvest the spiny plants.

A tryptamine derivative has been reported from *E. triglochidiatus* and it is one of the few cacti also thought to contain phenethylamines as well as tryptamine alkaloids.

Homalomena
Homalomena lauterbachii
Araceae
Other common names: Ereiba

Homalomena lauterbachii has already been mentioned in the earlier section about the tree known as agara, because it is traditionally mixed with this other herb by the indigenous people of Papua New Guinea. The leaves are the part that is required for the mixture, which produces an intoxicated state leading to visionary experiences and a deep slumber. These

Homalomena (Illustration: Aziz Ipsule)

leaves are oblong-lanceolate or cordate-ovate in form and are carried on short stems no more than 6in. high.

This species of Homalomena, and others in the genus, have pleasantly aromatic rhizomes, which have been utilised in folk medicine for the treatment of various complaints including skin problems. In Malaya an undisclosed part of one species is said to have been used in arrow poison. However, studies on the chemical makeup of this group of plants have not as yet revealed any known psychoactive substances.

I

Iboga
Tabernanthe iboga
Apocynaceae
Other common names: Eboga, Eboka

Iboga (Illustration: Aziz Ipsule)

The shrub *Tabernanthe iboga*, commonly known as iboga, is a native of the equatorial jungles in the Congo and Gabon parts of Africa but the hallucinogen and stimulant ibogaine that it contains has become well known worldwide.

The plant grows to between 4 and 5ft. in height and has ovate leaves about 4in. long. It is a typical herb of the forest undergrowth but is also deliberately cultivated near the homes of the native people. Iboga bears tiny yellowish, pinkish or white and pink spotted flowers in sprays of between 5 and 12 and these blooms are followed by pointed egg-shaped yellow-orange-coloured fruit the size of olives. These fruit are sweet to taste and edible containing no hallucinogenic or stimulant properties. The whole plant yields copious and vile-smelling white latex. Besides ibogaine, the plant also contains many other alkaloids with 6% of mixed indole alkaloids found in the bark of its roots. The psychoactive alkaloid ibogaine in low doses acts as a stimulant but at higher amounts has hallucinogenic properties. It is taken as a tea made from the dried powdered root bark or by chewing it. About 2 or 3 teaspoons of the powdered bark is usual as a low dose for women and 3 to 5 spoons for men, but much larger amounts up to 300 and 1,000g. Have been used in ceremonies to 'break open the head'. In low doses it is also very popular as an aphrodisiac and it is reported that it can cure impotency. Iboga users claim that they can engage in sexual activity for as long as 6 hours and upwards to as much as 17 hours. Ibogaine increases both endurance limits and muscular strength as these people would testify. A report from as early as 1864 states that 'warriors and hunters use it constantly to keep themselves awake during night watches'.It was also popular before lion hunts to keep the huntsmen alert. In fact, iboga is said to be able to give those who consume it for such purposes, the ability to stay awake and stand motionless for up to 2 days, all the while waiting for a lion to cross their pathway. In the 1880s, according to information received from informants in the Gabon area, the German colonials had allowed and even encouraged the moderate use of iboga by the men working on hard labouring projects like the Douala (Yaounde railroad).

In much larger doses the drug ibogaine is classed as a ritual hallucinogen and is used in a shamanic way by the Fang tribe from Gabon who founded the Bwiti cult. There is also the similar Mbiri cult. The members of these cults meet at night and engage in religious activities to do with the worship and belief in 'Nyingwan Mebege', the feminine or goddess principle of the universe. The participants also feel that they are in touch with their ancestors, and part of the focus is to give its members a taste of the world beyond this one, the world of the afterlife and the spirits. Dancers, energised by the herb's stimulant properties, are known to keep going all night to the rhythmic drumming of the tribal musicians.

Some of the imagery used by the cults has been taken from Catholicism fused with the old ancestor-based religions, for example, the cult-members hold their meetings and services in chapels, where they seek to achieve the state of 'nlem mvore', meaning 'one-heartedness'. Followers of the Bwiti cult are called 'ndzi eboga', which means eboga eater. The ideas expressed by this religious movement, together with the use of iboga, have spread amongst the tribes, and in many ways, this appears to be a backlash at the attempts by missionaries to make the people into Christians. It has provided a strong and timely sense of unity amongst these people in a world where outside influences have threatened the very fabric of traditional society and culture.

There is a 6-stage initiatory system for these 'eboga eaters' and the high dosages of the herb ingested by participants seeking initiation, often enters the level of dangerously toxic. Very large doses of ibogaine can produce convulsions, respiratory failure and death. In fact, cases of manslaughter and murder have been brought against cult-leaders following the deaths of initiates who had taken the herb. However, it must be pointed out that these leaders are well aware of the dangers of ingestion of large amounts of the herb and never encourage its use in such high dosages outside the practice of initiation.

The first stage of the initiation ceremony is when the would-be initiate is met by the leaders who assess whether he or she is deemed ready, and sometimes this meeting involves the use of a small amount of iboga being administered to the initiate. On the next occasion, and if the candidate is accepted, consumption of the sacred herb is kept up all day long and in high dosages, all within the confines of the chapel. The third stage is reached when the suitably intoxicated initiate is taken out into the jungle for ritual preparation, before returning to the congregation at the place of worship. Here the initiate must join in the ceremonies while continuing to take more iboga. At around midnight the person being initiated has usually reached such a high level of intoxication that they collapse. This marks the fourth stage and signifies the entry to the land of the dead. No further iboga is given to the initiate after this and the fifth stage requires that the fully intoxicated initiate is taken out of the chapel again into an environment where they will not be disturbed. Here they are left to complete their initiatory experience. The final stage takes place the following morning when the initiate has had time to recover from their trance and is able to talk about their experience to other members of the tribe. This ritual clearly expresses the idea of death and rebirth and the participants paint themselves white with kaolin to signify the colour of the spirits, who are generally believed to be this colour. Because the cult leaders are controlling the settings and imagery fed to the initiates, the reported visions are often very similar. This, of course, adds to the unification engendered between the tribes that may well in the past have been at war with one another. So iboga brings peace between tribal people.

A close relative of iboga is the Australian ibogaine bush or iodine bush with the botanical name of *Tabernaemontana orientalis*. The indole alkaloid ibogaine is again present in this species, although the Aborigines appear to have only used this bush for medicinal purposes.

Ibogaine is a Schedule 1 prohibited drug in America and this illegal status is extended to the plant. However, despite its illegality in the US, ibogaine has been used successfully to get drug addicts to quit their addictions in clinics in Mexico and other parts of the world. Ibogaine is being hailed as a new and alternative treatment for addiction to heroin, cocaine, alcohol and other drugs, for those who can afford it. It has become the subject of an alternative medical subculture for the treatment of drug addiction. It seems crazy that a drug that can get hard drug addicts off these substances should be illegal in many places, but sadly this is how it is.

J

Justicia
Justicia pectoralis
Acanthaceae
Other common names: Tilo, Chapantye, Curia, Freshcut, Death-angel, Mashi-Hiri

Justicia pectoralis is a Central and South American herb that can grow to 200 cm in height, and bears pink or white flowers arising from its stems which have a tendency to spread out and root at the nodes. It is a common weed of the Caribbean and in most parts of tropical America, where it is found growing on roadsides and in waste ground, as well as on sandy soil in lowland forests. It is traditionally used in herbal medicine as a relaxant and tonic, and has a pleasantly aromatic smell due to the coumarin it produces. The plant also contains umbelliferone. *Justicia pectoralis* is used as a treatment for stomach aches, headaches, coughs, colds and flu, and as a hair rinse.

Justicia pectoralis var. *stenophylla* is regarded as an entheogen by some Brazilian tribal shamans, and it is added to ingredients used to brew ayahuasca. The Krahós call the plant 'mashi-hiri', and think of it as such a potent plant that it should not be used by the uninitiated. Besides being an admixture for making ayahuasca brews, *Justicia pectoralis* var. *stenophylla* is added to virola snuffs that are used by shamans for hallucinogenic purposes and will be covered in more detail later in this volume.

K

Kava Kava
Piper methysticum
Piperaceae
Other common names: Ava, Ava pepper, Intoxicating Pepper,
Kava, Keu, Yangona

Kava kava is a tall perennial shrub reaching heights of 6 to 10ft.
or more. It is native to Polynesia, the Sandwich Islands, Solomon
Islands, Tahiti, Fiji, Samoa, Hawaii, New Guinea, and official in
the Australian colonies. The plant has heart-shaped leaves and
dense flowering spikes of white flowers. These flowers are male
or female.

The native islanders of the places where it grows prepare
a narcotic drink from the stump of the stem together with the
rootstock. This is done by pounding or grinding these parts of
the plant and soaking them in cold water, although to work
well some form of oil needs adding to make an emulsion
because the psychoactive ingredients are not soluble in water.
The active substances in kava kava are grouped together as
kavalactones, and are technically known as the resinous alpha
pyrones yangonin, dihydroyangonin, kawain, dihydrokawain,
methysticin and dihydromethysticin. Chewing and spitting out
of the masticated root by the women and children is a commonly
used method of preparing kava kava. The mixing of the root
with the alkaline saliva helps the breakdown process along and
seems to release the active constituents. This is known as the
'Tonga method' as opposed to the 'Fiji method', which grinds
and bruises the root between rocks. The resulting juice is hot
to the taste and mixed with coconut milk is intoxicating as it is,
but Westerners may well resort to lecithin or salad oil bought
from the health store. The finished beverage is a dirty-brown or
greyish liquid and quite bitter, as well as hot to the taste.

In Hawaii, kava kava is drunk by the nobles for recreational purposes, by the priests for religious ceremonies and by the rest of the people as an aid to relaxation. Kava kava was once tried by the UK's Queen on her Jubilee visit to Samoa in 1977, on the occasion of the island King's kava ceremony. Shamans who use the herb claim that it assists their psychic powers and 'kahuna' seers read the bubbles of a brew as a means of divination. One of the first effects noticed is that the mouth goes tingly and numb like the sensation produced by a dental anaesthetic. This quickly fades and a feeling of tranquillity takes over the body that has been described as 'like lying in a bed of rose petals'. Generally kava kava causes a state of euphoria and relaxation, and some people claim it also gives an increase in mental clarity and perception. The herb also has soporific qualities and the kava kava imbiber may fall asleep under its influence. Drs. Schultes and Hofmann have actually classed kava kava as a hypnotic, stating clearly that it is not a hallucinogen. However, the herb is classified, many people think it is superior to alcohol and kava kava bars sprung up in the Pacific Islands to take advantage of its popularity and as an alternative to the usual type of drinking establishment. Kava kava has become such an integral part of the culture of the Pacific Islanders that these people are able to classify the herb into an astonishing number of varieties. In Vanuatu alone, the people there recognise some 247 types. According to the Erowid Psychoactive Vaults website, the Fijians cultivate 5 varieties with 3 white types and 2 black. The black types of kava kava are considered faster growers and are used as a commercial crop, and with the white form it is the roots that are harvested for personal use. These varieties are known as 'kasa'. 'Kasa Leva' is the black type, and 'Kasa Balavu' denotes the white.

The use of kava kava can have adverse effects because too much of it can lead to blurred vision and unsteady gait. Over a long period of regular use it can cause skin problems.

Nevertheless, Kava kava has been cultivated and used by

the Polynesian Islanders for around 3,000 years, and this has been evidenced by the results of research conducted on the island nation of Vanuatu, which was once known as the New Hebrides. Elsewhere on the Eloaua Island, north of the Bismarck Archipelago of Papua, a part of a fossilised stem was discovered along with a style of decorated pottery known as Lapita. The Lapita people are considered to be the ancestors of the modern Polynesians and this pottery example could well be evidence of a very early drinking utensil used for imbibing kava kava. Elaborately carved and decorated drinking vessels are very much part of the culture associated with using kava kava today, and this could easily be a follow on from earlier Lapita customs.

Kava kava is used medicinally as an anaesthetic, an antiseptic, and as a diuretic. It is used as a treatment for venereal and urinary disease, as well as for gout, rheumatism and bronchial infections. Some people have claimed that kava kava works as an aphrodisiac that enhances sexual activity but others claim the reverse and that it deadens such feelings. A case of different strokes for different folks it seems!

Kava kava was once sold as a natural high, and there was even a psychedelic rock band named Kava Kava after the herb. It became widely marketed by health stores and by firms that produce vitamin, mineral and herbal supplements. However, since 13 January 2003 it has been illegal to sell, supply or import kava kava in the UK. The reason given for this ban was that kava kava was dangerous because it could potentially cause damage to the liver. It was not proven conclusively that kava kava was a danger but if it could cause harm it was too much of a risk for the UK to take. Canada, Switzerland and Germany are among the other countries where it has also been made illegal. Kava kava has become one more herb that is against the law in 'Nanny State' Britain today.

Khat
Catha edulis
Celastraceae
Other common names: Abyssinian Tea, African Tea, Arabian Tea, Cat, Catha, Chat, Kat, Miraa, Qat

Khat is an evergreen shrub or small tree bearing shiny elliptical leaves that have slightly serrated edges and small insignificant whitish flowers, which have 5 petals and are formed in the axils along the stems. Khat is a native of most of the northern part of Africa, including Ethiopia, the Yemen, Kenya and Somalia, and it is also found in Afghanistan and Turkestan. The tree likes a well-drained and sunny position but is sensitive to droughts and frost-tender. If kept too wet it is susceptible to fungal attacks. Khat can be propagated by cuttings or from seed, and there is more than one variety of the shrub with some types being easier to cultivate than others.

Khat is a stimulant and owes most of its effects to a substance called cathinone. This alkaloid is similar to ephedrine and can be nearly as potent as an amphetamine if enough is taken. Khat also contains various other substances such as cathidine, celastrin and ratine. As a stimulant, khat is ingested by chewing the fresh leaves and/or the young green twigs. The lower more mature leaves are stronger than the young ones. It is usual for the khat-user to chew the leaves slowly, holding the mass of leaves in the cheek and adding fresh ones. This process allows the cathinone to leach out. The plant must be fresh or the active substances in it drastically lose their potency, and after only 1 or 2 days may be no good. This means that shipments of the plant had to be transported by air from countries where it grows to a ready market elsewhere. Khat is traditionally harvested in the morning before the heat has built up and the leaves and twigs are bundled together and wrapped in large leaves like those of the banana to keep them fresh.

K

Because the khat plant comes from predominantly Muslim countries it has become a big part of this culture, a religious culture that forbids alcohol, cannabis and other intoxicants. It is mainly consumed by men and is actually believed to be a gift from Allah, who, in ancient times, is said to have given the herb to a monk to help him endure his long nights of prayer. It is often combined with coffee drinking and the two stimulants appear to have a synergistic effect.

In British cities where there are large Somali communities, khat was on sale in shops and at markets, though this has all been stopped because the herb was classified as an illegal Class C drug, as of 24 June 2014. This followed complaints that the use of the herb could cause psychosis and mental illness. The World Health Organisation had already classified it in 1980 as a drug of abuse that can cause mild to moderate psychological dependence. Many businesses have been destroyed in the Yemen and elsewhere where the plant is harvested and transported for supply. It was a cash crop for many farmers and a lot of people have lost their livelihoods due to the ban. Businesses in the UK involved with the importing of khat have had to close as well. It is not just Britain that has made khat illegal because the plant is classed as a drug and has illegal status in many other countries, including Germany, Canada and the US.

M

Maguey
Agave americana
Asparagaceae
Other common names: American Aloe, Century Plant, Mescale, Tacamba

The century plant or maguey is a very large species of the *Agave* genus of succulents. It forms a rosette of grey-green very spiky leaves which can reach about 6ft. in height and may be 6–10in. in width. These leaves have additional armour in the form of sharp hooked spines along their edges. After 10–25 years of growth in good circumstances, a single inflorescence is produced which can attain a height of as much as 15–20ft., and greenish or white bell-shaped flowers are carried on its branches. After flowering, the plant dies leaving many small rosette plantlets and offshoots to carry on. The name century plant refers to the notion that the plant only flowers after 100 years, and, indeed, in cold climates it does take very many years before it bears blooms. The maguey is semi-hardy and can withstand a light frost if kept dry. It also stands up well to droughts and wildfires. It likes a very sunny location and well-drained sandy soil. Maguey is often grown as a spectacular ornamental plant in large containers or as a showpiece in summer bedding displays. There is a variegated strain of the plant with yellowish edges to the leaves.

In Mexico, maguey has been used to make an inebriating drink known as 'octli', 'metl', or 'pulque'. Other entheogens, such as datura, peyote and morning glories are often added to give extra 'kick' and psychoactive effect to brews made from it. Maguey was believed by the Aztecs to be the home of their goddess Mayahuel. Mexican tribes still use the plant as a medicine and for shamanic purposes. The leaves are fashioned into protective amulets and also attached to places of dwelling as a magical source of protection against evil in all its forms.

Maguey sap contains about 8% agavose (a sugar), hecogenin, oxalic acid, papain, saponin, and an essential oil.

Mammillaria cacti
Mammillaria craigii, M. grahamii, M. heyderi, M.senilis
Cactaceae
Other common names: Pincushion Cactus, Hikuri, False Peyote, Peyotillo, Peyote de San Pedro, Wichikuri

The *Mammillaria* cacti species named above have been called 'false peyotes' and are used as hallucinogens and for shamanic purposes by the Tarahumara Indians of Mexico, who are renowned for the ability as runners. All of the *Mammillaria* species are short round cacti with many spines. The species *craigii* has rose-coloured flowers, while those of *grahamii* are a violet colour, sometimes with white edges. *Heyderi* produces brilliant red flowers with iridescent centres and is one of the spiniest species. *M. craigii* is split open by the Indians to reveal the central tissue, which is sometimes roasted as part of the preparation. The top of the plant has its spines removed and is thought to be the most powerful part for its psychoactive properties. The tryptamine N-methyl3, 4-di-methoxyphenethylamine has been isolated from *M. heyderi,* a close relative of *M. craigii.* The intoxication produced by this species is said to cause a deep sleep in which the sleeper feels that they travel far, and also they may experience seeing brilliant colours.

The *Mammillaria* species are attractive and easy to propagate and very popular with collectors of cacti and succulents. For this reason most types are readily available from garden centres and nurseries around the world.

Mescal Bean
Sophora secundiflora
Fabaceae
Other common names: Coral Bean, Colorines, Frijoles, Red Beans

The orange-red or maroon beans of this representative of the very large pea and bean family may be known as mescal beans but they bear no resemblance chemically to the hallucinogenic mescaline or the fermented drink mescal. These seeds are very toxic and are no longer in use as an inebriant employed for shamanic purposes, although they were once used this way by various tribes, including the Chiricahua and the Mescalero Apache. Although the tree and its beans formed the basis of the 'Red Bean Cult' of the Plains Indians of the Rio Grande area this was superseded by the arrival of the safe peyote cactus as a popular psychoactive intoxicant and hallucinogen.

Some tribes gave the beans to their horses as a medicine and stimulant. Many tribes used the beans for their ornamental value in necklaces and other jewellery and to decorate their clothes.

The small tree or shrub the beans come from is found growing wild in Mexico, New Mexico and parts of Texas. It is an evergreen. It bears beautiful and fragrant violet-blue flowers in drooping racemes about 4in. long. These flowers are followed by hard woody pods containing 2–8 beans and these pods may well remain on the shrub for several seasons.

The alkaloids the mescal bean contains are all of the quinolzidine variety and are cystisine, N-methylcystisine and sparteine. Cystisine, which is chemically similar and in its action to nicotine, is very dangerous and can cause violent headaches, vomiting, heart trouble, convulsions, stupor and death. It is not a hallucinogen in the normal sense of the term, but ingested, its toxicity can produce a delirium. It is such a powerful poison that even the Indians who risked it only used one quarter of a roasted bean as a ritual dose, and the beans are less than 1in. big. Its effects can last for up to three days and may well result in a very long period of sleep. It is a sleep the user may not awaken from!

Mexican Buckeye
Ugnandia speciosa
Sapindaceae
Other common names: Texas Buckeye

The Texas buckeye is a large shrub or small tree that usually reaches about 6ft. but may in exceptional circumstances attain 30ft. in height. It is found on grassy hillsides in Texas and also in Mexico. The tree has pinnate leaves similar to those of the ash (*Fraxinus*) but serrated at the edges. The flowers are pinkish-purple and strongly perfumed. After the flowers have finished the Mexican buckeye produces leathery fruit about 2in. long and containing round, shiny black seeds.

According to Schultes and Hoffmann, in their *Plants of the Gods*, these seeds may once have been used for shamanic purposes, possibly in combination with other hallucinogens. In particular, peyote and the mescal bean have both been found in association with the Mexican buckeye by archaeological researchers. The seeds contain cyanogenic substances, and these types of compounds, although often toxic, have proven psychoactive in various other species of plant like the hydrangea, for example.

Mexican Poppy
Argemone mexicana, A. polyanthemos
Papaveraceae
Other common names: Chicalote, Devil's Fig, Prickly Poppy, Thistle Poppy, Flowering Thistle

The Mexican poppy is an annual herb that grows to a couple of feet in height in very good conditions but can be a lot smaller. It produces pretty yellow-petalled flowers and bluish-green spiny leaves. It likes a very sunny position but is quite hardy and besides Mexico it is also found in North and South America, as well as various subtropical and tropical countries throughout the world where it has spread as a weed.

Being a relative of its more notorious cousin the opium poppy (*Papaver somniferum*) it perhaps comes as no surprise to learn that the Mexican poppy also has narcotic properties. The leaves, stalks and flowers contain the alkaloids oxyberberine and proptopine, the root contains coptesine, sanguinarine is found in the seeds, while argemonine is produced by the foliage. These alkaloids make up only about 0.1% of the herb's contents but are strong enough to produce a narcotic effect. If inhaled as smoke the herb has a similar sedative and analgesic effect to the opium poppy, and may also induce a euphoric state in the smoker. The closely related *A. polyanthemos* is reported as having very similar properties to the Mexican poppy.

Morning Glory
Ipomoea tricolor
Convolvulaceae
Other common names: Badoh Negro, Badungas, Blue Star, Flying Saucers, Glory Seeds, Heavenly Blue, Pearly Gates, Pearly Whites, Piule, Seeds, Summer Skies, Tlililtzen, Wedding Bells, Yaxce'lil

The morning glory is such an attractive climbing plant that it is well known to gardeners all over the world. Although it is native to Mexico and Guatemala, it grows wild in other tropical and semitropical parts of America, and in summer is cultivated as an annual in parks and gardens in many temperate climes where it may be started under glass or indoors. The morning glory comes in a wide range of colours from blue or violet-blue to purple and also in white, and in the case of the variety known as Flying Saucers, with a mixture of blue or purplish and white

Heavenly Blue (Photo: Tim Brett)

in the same flowers. The flowers are funnel-shaped or trumpet-shaped and are like large versions of common bindweed flowers. As a point of interest, there are various other psychoactive herbs with flowers this shape, with the *Datura* and *Brugmansia* species being good examples. The morning glory also bears attractive, fairly large heart-shaped leaves, which complement the flowers really well, and a full-grown morning glory in full bloom, and rambling its way over a fence or trellis is a real picture!

Morning glories have been widely used shamanically by several Indian tribes, including the Chinantec and Mazatecs, who call the plant 'piule', and the Zapotecs who refer to this climbing herb as 'badoh negro'. The ancient Aztecs knew the morning glory as 'tlililtzen', and all these tribal people esteemed the seeds of the plant as a very important entheogen used in divination and in magical rituals and religious ceremonies. Not surprisingly, the plant has found favour with many modern neo-shamans and hippies too because it contains lysergic acid amides concentrated in its seeds, making the plant the nearest thing to 'acid' you can buy legally at the gardening shop. Back in the tail-end of the 1960s the authorities and media ran many scare stories in an effort to stamp out the use of morning glory as a recreational drug and LSD substitute, even going as far as renaming the plant on seed-packets as *Ipomoea*.

The seeds and plant contain D-isolysergic acid amide, D-lysergic acid amide, chanoclavine, and lysergol, and produce a hallucinatory experience quite similar in many ways to that of the illegal and much more potent LSD. One seed is equivalent to 1 mic. of LSD, so anything from 50–300 seeds is a dose that can produce a psychedelic experience, although the mixture of alkaloids these seeds contain are often known to cause nausea and vomiting. Obviously the more one takes the worse these unpleasant side effects can be, and can influence the experience in a negative way. Some people do not get on well with morning glory seeds and only experience sickness. This has been attributed to protective coatings added by seed-supply firms, and has been thought to be a potential danger. While this is sometimes true, generally the nausea is due to alkaloids in the seeds without any additional toxins added. However, to be on the safe side if you are considering trying this entheogen, it is probably best to grow your own supply, or to get them from suppliers that can guarantee their seeds are 'untreated' with fungicides and pesticides.

Morning glory seeds, which are black or dark-brown and shaped like little almost triangular boats, need to be ground up finely or very well chewed to feel the effects of the psychoactive alkaloids. Because the lysergic acid amides are soluble in water, another way is to leave the seeds soaking for a day or two, and then strain and drink. The Zapotecs call the seeds of the morning glory 'la aja shnash', which translates as 'seed of the virgin', and a brew of the herb was traditionally prepared for the shaman by a young girl. The plant has become associated with the Virgin Mary, and looking at the pristine beauty of a newly opened Heavenly Blue, or a pure white pearly gates flower, bedecked in dew on a summer morning, it is easy to think how apt this association is.

'Mushroom Madness' (various species of fungi)

The term 'mushroom madness' has been given to a state of high excitement and uncontrollable behaviour exhibited at times among members of the native cultures of New Guinea. This 'mushroom madness' is characterised by mass frenzy and groups running madly, sometimes even killing in the process. The term has been adopted by writers on the subject of shamanism and entheogens, including Schultes and Hofmann, Richard Rudgley, and many more, to loosely describe such crazed behaviour thought to be caused by the consumption of several unidentified fungi found growing wild on the islands. These authors have suggested that the 'madness' may well be some form of religious rite or other cultural expression amongst these people and may not be attributable to mushrooms at all. R. G. Wasson and R. Heim wrote in a work of 1965, entitled *The 'Mushroom Madness' of the Kuma* that the strange social phenomenon's origins lay in 'mythology not mycology'. But previous to this, back in 1936, father William A. Ross described an outbreak of this 'madness' among the people of the Mount Hagen area. He stated that 'the wild mushroom called "nonda" makes the user temporarily insane. He flies into a fit of frenzy. Death is even known to have resulted from its use. It is used before going out to kill another native, or in times of great excitement, anger or sorrow'. Other cases have been reported among the festivities of the Sina-Sina people and among the rituals of the Bimin-Kuskusmin of New Guinea. The Bimin-Kuskusmin are known for definite to be users of psychoactives, including tobacco and hallucinogenic mushrooms, but the exact details of such usage and of their rituals remains very unclear.

Several species of fungi from different families have been suggested as potential entheogens used by these people and these are the mushrooms *Russula agglutina* (of the *Russulaceae*), *Heimiella angrieformis* and *H. retispora* (of the *Boletaceae*), and from the same family but different genus, the species *Boletus manicus* and *B. reayi*. Several species of *Russula* have caused documented cases of ibotenic acid and muscimole poisonings, and these substances are the deliriants responsible for hallucinogenic intoxication by the well-known fly agaric (*Amanita muscaria*).

Clearly much further research is needed on this matter, but one thing is for sure in any part of the world, that it is obviously a case of 'mushroom madness' to eat any fungi at all without being absolutely certain of their identification. Some mushrooms and toadstools are very toxic indeed and a simple mistake could mean your last meal.

N

Nutmeg
Myristica fragrans
Myristicaceae
Other common names: Mace, Nux moschata

Whole Nutmegs (Photo: Iolo Jones)

Nutmeg is a household word because it is such a commonly used spice that is an ingredient in countless sweets and savoury dishes all over the world, but what is not so commonly known is that in large doses it is an intoxicant and hallucinogen, and hence its inclusion here.

The nutmeg tree grows to about 25ft. in height and is native to the Banda Islands, Malayan Archipelago, and Moluccan Islands, as well as being cultivated in Sumatra and French Guiana. It is a handsome tree with dark green glossy leaves some 4–6in. in length and bearing small yellowish flowers in axillary racemes. The nutmeg tree is aromatic and readily yields a yellow juice from its grey-brown and smooth bark. The nutmeg carries its male and female flowers separately, although they look similar in appearance. The fruits that follow are much larger than the tiny flowers and consist of a globular drupe with a scarlet aril on the outside housing the whitish nutmeg kernel inside, and this 'nut' is mottled throughout with red-brown veins. When the nutmeg is harvested the arils are separated from the nuts and each part is collected and dried separately too. This is because the aril gives us the spice known as mace, and the nutmeg having a different flavour and appearance provides another product for the spice-rack. The nutmegs are dried and cured for several weeks over a very slow-burning fire and may also be sun-dried to start with. They are graded for quality and a good nutmeg should have a very distinctive fragrance, and a very strong and bitter warm and aromatic flavour. The mace should be in flexible cinnamon-yellow blades, either singles or double, and a warm yet aromatic taste.

Nutmeg has been used in herbal medicine against asthma and heart complaints and as a sedative in India, while Arabs have utilised the spice to help in cases of digestive disorder and also value it as an aphrodisiac. The famous English herbalist Nicholas Culpeper prescribed it for insomnia and against delirium (the very thing it can also cause!), while William Salmon, on the other hand and in agreement with Arab physicians, claimed that the oil rubbed on the genitals excited passions.

In *Potter's New Encyclopedia of Botanical Drugs and Preparations*, nutmeg is described as being used as a remedy for flatulence, nausea and actual vomiting. It further states that Joseph Mill said of nutmegs: 'they are heating, drying and carminative, strengthen the stomach and bowels, stop vomiting, help digestion, comfort the head and nerves, cure the palpitation of the heart and prevent swooning, and are of service against vapors'.

Nutmeg is credited with magical properties too and is one of the ingredients used in the recipe for a perfume described in that much sought-after grimoire *The Key of Solomon*.

Already known in India as a 'narcotic fruit', its psychoactive properties became well known in the underworld of America and Europe many years later. However, in general, it has never been a popular substance of recreational abuse because the amount you need to get a hallucinatory state is also close to a dangerous and most unpleasant overdose. Approximately 10 gm is required as a minimum dose or a small matchbox full (between 1 and 2 ground nutmegs), although a level teaspoonful of nutmeg powder will usually do the trick. A large degree of nausea and also diarrhoea may be experienced, and other unpleasant side effects are dizziness and panic, flushes, parched mouth, palpitations, bloodshot eyes and difficulty in urination. A drunken feeling and auditory distortions of time and space may occur and the whole experience may continue for as much as 12 hours, followed by a very bad hangover with aching muscles and a totally burnt out feeling for up to 2 days afterwards. Too much will definitely cause a very unpleasant experience and may cause severe damage to the liver, which may even result in death from eventual organ failure. Nutmeg has been a substance used by prisoners, sailors, struggling musicians and artists, and anyone unable to get or buy anything better. Having said all that, the legendary jazz saxophonist Charlie 'Bird' Parker is reported to have introduced the stuff to his band and fellow musicians as a cheap legal way of getting high.

In 1946, the political activist Malcolm X, before his conversion to the Muslim religion, was a regular user of nutmeg in prison whenever his supply of marijuana ran out. In his autobiography he wrote: 'I first got high in Charlestown on nutmeg ... stirred into a glass of cold water, a penny matchbox full of nutmeg had the kick of three or four reefers.'

The aromatic oil of nutmeg contains 9 components belonging to the terpenes and the aromatic ethers. The major constituent and active ingredient is the terpene myristicin, and although it has been thought to be responsible for the psychoactive effects, this may be only partially true because it is known to act as an irritant. The aromatic ether safrole is another likely candidate for the hallucinogenic effects. Whatever the truth may be on this matter, it seems clear that the best place for using the spices nutmeg and mace is actually in the place they are known best from, namely the kitchen, as a delicious spice and fragrance for various desserts and confections.

O

Ololiuqui
Turbina corymbosa
Convolvulaceae
Other common names: Badoh, Christmaspops, Christmas Vine,
Flower of the Virgin, Little Children, Round Things, Snake Plant

Ololiuqui (Illustration: Aziz Ipsule)

Ololiuqui is yet another psychoactive vine from the convolvulus
family, and like its close relatives the morning glories, it contains
lysergic acid amides. The plant is a large woody climber with
heart-shaped leaves and many-flowered cymes bearing the
white flowers with greenish stripes dividing the funnel-shaped
corollas. The fruit contains a single hard brown seed, which is

round like one of the plant's common names suggests. Ololiuqui is found growing in Mexico and Central America, as well as other tropical areas of North and South America.

It has a long history of use by the shamans of many Indian tribes including the Chinantec, the Mazatec, the Mixtec, and the Zapotec, and is still commonly used today. The ancient Mayans and Aztecs also regarded this as a very sacred herb and used the seeds in their ceremonies and as a hallucinogen.

About 15 crushed seeds are soaked in water and the strained liquid is drunk. It is best consumed on an empty stomach or nausea is likely. Indian shamans believed that the seeds are best collected by the person seeking healing or other help, and that they should be ground up by a virgin. The drink, when it is ready, is consumed at night in a quiet place where there will be no disturbance. It is considered very similar but superior to the morning glory.

Orchids
Oncidium cebolleta
Orchidaceae
Other common names: Cebolleta

The tropical orchid species *Oncidium cebolleta* is an epiphyte and is found growing on trees and also on cliffs in the Tarahumara area of Mexico, as well as in other parts of Central America, South America and Florida in the north. According to Schultes and Hofmann, this species is suspected of being psychoactive and to have been used as a substitute for peyote in times of scarcity. Although an alkaloid has been found in the orchid very little else is known regarding its potential for usage for shamanic purposes.

The plant has a pseudo bulb at the base from which the fleshy grey-green leaves arise and these are often dotted with purple. So too, is the flowering stalk, which is also spotted with purplish-brown. Keeping this theme going, the flowers have brownish-yellow sepals and petals also spotted with darker blotches. A 3-lobed lip under an inch long is bright yellow with reddish-brown marks. Altogether it is a very unusual and attractive flower with an exotic appearance, so typical of the orchid family.

P

Pancratium
Pancratium trianthum
Amaryllidaceae
Other common names: Kwashi

Pancratium (Illustration: Aziz Ipsule)

Pancratium trianthum is one of a genus of 15 species, all of which are known as toxic. Many species are poisonous to the heart, others are emetics, and one causes death by paralysis of the central nervous system. *P. trianthum* is one of the more toxic types. Nevertheless, the Bushmen of Dobe in Botswana are said to use the plant as a hallucinogen by rubbing the sliced bulb over self-inflicted cuts to the head.

The flowers are greenish-white or white and are carried by the plant at the same time as the long grass-like leaves, all of which arise from the bulb below. The seeds are black and angled.

The species P. maritimum, a semi-hardy evergreen plant from the Mediterranean coastal area, is commonly known as the sea daffodil and grown as a garden flower.

Peyote
Lophophora williamsii, L. diffusa
Cactaceae
Other common names: Anhalonium, Anahalonium Lewinii, Echinocactus Williamsii, Hikori, Huatari, Mescal, Mescal Buttons, Muscal Buttons, Pellote, Peyotyl, Seni, Wakowi

Peyote (Photo: Iolo Jones)

No book on shamanic herbs would be complete without covering *Lophophora williiamsii* one of the most well-known psychoactive plants in the world. Bearing this in mind, and because this sacred cactus has links to so many other herbs and related issues covered in this book, I have decided to amend and add some fresh material and then to re-publish from my chapter on peyote in my first volume – *Herbs of the Northern Shaman*. So, once again, here are my findings on peyote:

The peyote cactus, with its main active alkaloid mescaline, has rivalled LSD as one of the most potent mind-altering substances around. The two species named above are both true botanical oddities and grow wild in the dry, stony desert ground of Texas and Mexico but are becoming increasingly rare and threatened with extinction due to over-collection and harvesting by unscrupulous collectors.

Peyote is one of the very few spineless varieties among some two thousand different types of cactus found growing in the world. The 'peyote button' consists of a bluish or greyish-green succulent pincushion with a tuft of furry wool-like fluff in the middle. The word 'peyote' is derived from the Nahuatl language meaning 'cocoon-silk'. From this tuft emerges the pink-coloured flower, followed by the fleshy seedpod containing several tiny black seeds. The cactus grows outward and downward and as one flower goes to seed it starts to move away from the centre and goes downward to be replaced by a new one and the cycle starts again. The whole peyote button is only a small part of the plant, which has a large carrot-like taproot underground.

Peyote (Illustration: Janice Pugsley)

The cactus is very slow growing indeed and can take as much as thirteen years to mature. It is partially due to this long period of time necessary for its growth that it is faring so badly when collected from its wild habitat. The Native American tribes, having great reverence for the peyote cactus, have always collected what they needed with care but sadly this has not been the case in recent years with other people who have sought out this powerful psychoactive plant. Actually, if the button is carefully cut off from the root with a wooden knife then the rootstock below should be able to clone many more button clusters on top. These mass clusters can reach some 4 or 5 foot across and are regarded as especially powerful and sacred by the Huichol Indians. Individual plants never grow more than about four inches in diameter and increase by forming new plants at the base. The older the plants are, the more the respect that is shown for them by the Indians and these elderly cactus specimens are affectionately called 'Father' or 'Grandfather Peyote'.

While I was writing more to add to this section, a series called *The Last of the Medicine Men* was actually coming to an end on British BBC2 television. In this series, the presenter Benedict Allen travels far and wide around the globe meeting representatives of surviving shamanic cultures and finding out about their cultural traditions and beliefs. In a recent episode he went on pilgrimage with the Huichols of Mexico to search for peyote and to gather supplies of the sacred fungus. The programme illustrated clearly how important rituals are to shamanic people and also how much respect and reverence is attached to a power plant or sacred herb as well as for all living things. We are shown how they make personal sacrifices with regards to sticking to dieting restrictions and also how the members of the tribe must all publically confess sexual indiscretions. To symbolise the different world the peyote can show the participants, the leading shaman gives new names for all the objects in the world around them. These they must learn to show they are prepared to leave the old mundane world behind when entering the spiritual world shown by the cactus. Echoing what I have already said earlier, the programme also sadly showed how the tribe had great difficulty finding any of the peyote cacti, which was once so abundant in their traditional location for gathering it. When we see evidence like this for the very great threat to a species of plant-life we can also see how this is reflected in the equally threatened destruction of a whole culture and tribal society. Allen, himself, ingested some of the peyote that they did find and gets to become for a short while a part of this shamanic culture and to glimpse their way of interpreting the world. A book of the series exists and details of this are given in the appendices and bibliography section.

The Mexican Indians communed with their deities via the peyote cactus and when the Spanish conquistadors invaded the land they were not able to convince the natives that peyote was an 'evil' to be shunned. Countless Indians were horribly murdered in the name of Catholicism and the cross but the survivors incorporated elements of the Biblical imagery and belief into their own peyote-fuelled ceremonies, and, despite all the oppression of the Spaniards, news of the cactus and its powers spread swiftly northwards to other tribes of Central America and up into the North American continent. Foremost among the Indians who spread the use of peyote were the Mescalero Apaches and from them, by the late 1800s, it had become part and parcel of the religious practices of very many of the Plains Indian tribes. The Arapahoes, Comanche, Cheyenne, Delaware, Kiowas, Pawnees and Shawnees are all examples of peyote-eating tribes-people.

One of the most well-known Indians to be directly inspired by the peyote cactus was the Caddo-Delaware John Wilson, who was also known as Wovoka. Wilson had been a leader in the Ghost Dance movement of the Plains Indians and had learned of the cactus and its powers from a Comanche he had met. Wovoka went into the forest with his wife and consumed as many as fifteen peyote buttons a day for a fortnight. In the resulting peyote intoxication and shamanic trance he was 'continually translated in spirit to the sky realm where he was conducted by Peyote'. He was shown the 'road' leading 'from Christ's grave to the Moon in the Sky, which Christ had taken in his ascent'. In addition to this, Wovoka learned of many more teachings from Peyote, which were to form his pathway for the rest of his life. He was given details of ceremonies, special face-paintings that were to be worn and sacred songs that were to be sung.

Peyote is eaten raw or dried and sometimes taken brewed as a tea and is best consumed on an empty stomach. The Native American tribes who use it regard it as a 'hard road' and they often have far stronger constitutions for such herbal preparations than many people around today. They also have great respect for the cactus as a sacred plant and often fast or purify themselves before rituals in which it is taken. Some tribes believe that the person who is a partaker of the peyote cactus actually tastes his or her self. So, the purer they are the sweeter should be the taste. Having said that, many tribes have a tribal member who for the course of a ceremony is designated 'shovel man'. This person is responsible for dealing with any vomiting that occurs and providing cups or can for tribal members to spit into.

One of the reasons for this problem is the very large mixture of alkaloids the cactus contains, namely at least 40 phenethylamine and isoquinoline alkaloids. Besides mescaline there is lophophorine (like strychnine in its action and can cause unpleasant side effects besides being a respiratory stimulant), pelotine (a convulsant), anhalonine (a reflex excitant) and other alkaloids such as anhaline, anhalamine, anhalonidine, N-methylmescaline, N-acetylmescaline, O-methylanhalonidine and peyotline.

Mescaline, the main psychoactive constituent, is able to be extracted and isolated from the other alkaloids in the peyote cactus or synthesised. In the form of mescaline sulphate it was to impress author and novelist Aldous Huxley so much that it became the subject matter of his book *The Doors of Perception and Heaven and Hell*. This book is said to have provided the inspiration for the name of the late Jim Morrison's incredibly influential rock-band The Doors. Huxley had volunteered himself as a human guinea-pig for experimentation with the drug back in 1953 and on a lovely May morning in the Los Angeles hills he cleansed the doors of his own perception. The intensity of the experience was such that he wrote:

I became aware of a slow dance of golden lights. A little later there were sumptuous red surfaces swelling and expanding from bright nodes of energy that vibrated with a continuously changing, patterned life ... The books, for example, with which my study walls were lined ... glowed, when I looked at them, with brighter colours, a profounder significance. Red books, like rubies; emerald books; books bound in agate, of aquamarine, of yellow topaz; lapis lazuli books whose colour was so intense, so intrinsically meaningful, that they seemed to be on the point of leaving the shelves to thrust themselves more insistently on my attention.

Aldous Huxley's experiences with mescaline, as well as with LSD, caused him to regard these substances as extremely beneficial, almost as means of gaining 'enlightenment' and as a key to redemption for the human race. Like Timothy Leary he became a 'messiah for the psychedelic movement'.

Someone, who became very involved in this movement of the '60s is Elizabeth Gips. Elizabeth is currently an author and celebrated 'hippie elder'. She is also the presenter of a cult 'evolutionary' radio show called *Changes*. Her fascinating and uplifting tale is told in *Scrapbook of a Haight Ashbury Pilgrim*, published by Changes Press of Santa Cruz, California, and in it she says of a peyote trip: 'What a gift. The curtains waved through time, children looked like flowers on the merry-go-round in the park and licence plates on cars had cosmic meanings beyond meanings.'

The religious experience that peyote and mescaline could give to the user was, of course, as already detailed, well known to the Red Indian tribes long before Huxley's experiments, and, indeed, became the basis for the founding of the Native American Church of North America. This church was formed by the 1906 confederation of peyote-eating tribes and today has more than twenty-five thousand members throughout America and Canada. Because peyote forms the religious communion for the members of the church it was ruled that it was legal for these people to possess and consume the sacred cactus. The general populace, however, have no such rights and, indeed, peyote falls in the list of substances declared illegal by Schedule One of the Controlled Substances Act. Several American states have tried, unsuccessfully, to bring laws forbidding church members from partaking of the cactus too but they have failed in their efforts because such a law would be an unconstitutional violation of the Bill of Rights' guarantee of freedom of religion.

In the United Kingdom, at the time of writing, it is legal to grow and to sell the peyote cactus, although consumption of it is not allowed. It is also legal in the Netherlands, where several ethnobotanical supply firms cultivate the cactus and include the living plant in their catalogues.

There is a considerable amount of evidence that shows that the spread of peyote-eating was a great help to the Indians in combating alcoholism, which many had succumbed to, partly in an effort to ease the pain of the terrible destruction that had been brought to their land and culture. Very many Indians welcomed the peaceful 'love-button' peyote cactus instead of the damaging 'firewater'. The Native American peyote-users also found the cactus invaluable in treating all manner of ailments ranging from dandruff to a treatment for wounds and serious illness such as cancer. Many Indians believe that they owe their good health to a life of using peyote as a sacrament. Even tribes who oppose its use for religious purposes grant that it is an invaluable tool in the battle against disease. Frank Takes Gun, national president of the Native American Church had this to say about the cactus:

At fourteen, I first used Father Peyote. This was on the Crow Reservation in Montana, and I was proud to know that my people had a medicine that was God-powerful. Listen to me, peyote does have many amazing powers. I have seen a blind boy regain his sight from taking it. Indians with ailments that hospital doctors couldn't cure have become healthy again after a peyote meeting.

The species *diffusa* is a different shade of green, often being a yellowish-green in colour and also it has much larger flowers, which are white. It is called a 'false peyote' or 'peyotl' and is regarded by some Indians as having noxious effects. This cactus does not contain the same balance of alkaloids as the true peyote and the main active constituent is reported to be pellotine or peyotline

Several other cacti found throughout the Americas contain mescaline-like substances and one of these, the Donána, is covered earlier on in my first book. The San Pedro *(Trichocereus pachanoi)*, the Peruvian Torch *(T. peruvianus)* and related species from the South American Andes, contain mescaline itself and are used by the people there for similar shamanic and healing properties.

Like a few other psychoactive herbs covered in this book, the peyote cactus has found its way into movie scripts and onto the big screen. In Jim Jarmusch's *Dead Man*, Johnny Depp stars as Blake, a young man who ends up being shot following an incident in a town he was visiting whilst seeking a job. Mortally wounded and fleeing the town, Blake is found by an American Indian travelling in the area. On discovering the injured man's name, the Indian rescuer decides that this Blake is the visionary

P

Peruvian Torch (Photo: Steve Andrews)

English poet with the same surname. The Indian is known as Nobody and he acts as a guide and companion to the dying Blake, whom he believes is the great poet he has studied and felt a considerable affinity for. In the course of their journey, Nobody partakes of 'Grandfather Peyote' and introduces his friend to it. On screen we see a vision of Depp's face transformed into a skull. The film shows how Blake becomes more and more in tune with Mother Earth and his Indian friend's ways as he dies out of his life as a white man in a corrupt and decadent west.

Peyote Cimarrón
Ariocarpus fissuratus, A. retusus
Cactaceae
Other common names: Chaute, Chautle, Hikuli Sunamé, Living
Rock, Tsunami, Tsuwiri, Dry Whisky

Peyote Cimarron (Illustration: Aziz Ipsule)

The Mexican Tarahumara tribe regards these cacti as 'false
peyotes', like the species before, however, they also claim that
the plants may be more powerful than the true peyote. The
species *retusus* is called 'tsuwiri' in Huichol meaning 'false
peyote' and this tribe believe, that if a person, who is seeking
peyote has not been properly purified, then he will be led astray
by the 'false peyote'. And further to this belief, that if he finds it
and consumes it then he will become insane.

The species *A. fissuratus* is known as 'tsunami' and also among
some tribes as 'chaute', which means 'living rock'. Naturally,
with so many species identified as 'false peyotes' or 'living rocks'
there is plenty of room for confusion when it comes to trying to
present the correct details. This species, in particular, is thought
to be more potent than peyote, which, if it is true, certainly takes
some doing! To confuse things further there are two varieties of

this cactus: *A. fissuratus var. lloydii* and *A. fissuratus var. fissuratus* but it is reported that their chemical makeup and alkaloid content is very similar. The cacti contain for the most part the alkaloid hordenine and to a lesser degree N-methyltyramine and N-methyl-3, 4-dimethoxy-B-phenethylamine. *A. Kotschoubeyanus* and *A. trigonus* both also contain this mixture of alkaloids and therefore, are psychoactive too.

All the cacti in this family are small and greyish-green or brownish in colour with characteristic 3-angled tubercules and dense masses of hair in the spaces, known as areoles, between. The largest cactus specimens only reach some 6in. in diameter and are so low-growing and disguised by their colouration and form that, when not in bloom, they are very difficult to spot in the barren and sandy areas in which they grow. The flowers are either pink or white or purplish depending on the variety and species. *A. trigonus* has yellowish flowers, however. The *Ariocarpus* cacti are all endangered species in the wild and are covered by protection laws. Seeds, however, can be obtained from cactus specialists, horticultural suppliers and ethnobotanical catalogues.

Peyotillo
Pelecyphora aselliformis
Cactaceae
Other common names: Hatchet cactus

Pelecyphora aselliformis is another of the 'false peyotes' and is called 'peyotillo' in Mexico where it is found growing in the area around San Luis Potosi and elsewhere. Very little else is known about it with regard to its possible shamanic uses by the Mexican Indians apart from the fact that it is recognised as belonging to this group of cacti.

It is a very distinctive and beautiful cactus with a cylindrical solitary grey-green body from which the stunning bell-shaped flowers are formed. These are just over 1in. across and have contrasting outer segments of white with the inner petals a deep pink colour.

Alkaloids have been found in studies of the plant but further research is necessary. According to Gareth Rose, in his booklet *The Psychedelics Volume 3 Psychedelic Cacti,* the plant is known as the hatchet cactus because it bears oddly flattened tubercules resembling the tool in question. He also informs readers of the details of alkaloids discovered in peyotillo cactus. There are minute traces of mescaline, too little to have any effect, and small quantities of anhaladine, anhalidine, hordenine, N-methylmescaline, pellotine, 3-dimethyltrichocereine, B-phenethylamine, N-methyl-B-phenethylamine, 3,4-dimethoxy-B-phenethylamine, N-methyl-3,4-dimethoxy-B-phenethylamine and 4-methoxy-B-phenethylamine. Most of these alkaloids and phenethylamines are also found in the peyote cactus but in much larger quantities. Despite the small quantities of mescaline found in this cactus, some suppliers have sold it as a mescaline-containing species.

Piule
Rhynchosia phaseoloides, R. longeracemosa, R. pyramidalis
Fabaceae

As I stated in the introduction to this book, all of today's ethnobotanists are indebted to the work of Schultes and Hofmann. Once again, it was these authors who brought to our attention the possibility that several types of *Rhynchosia,* with their very decorative beans, may well have been employed for shamanic purposes by the Native Americans of Mexico. They cite as evidence the fact that frescoes were found at Tepantitla, dated 300–400 CE, showing paintings, which seem to depict these seeds. Also, a name from a tribe from Oaxaca given to the beans is 'piule', which is the word they used for the seeds of

Rivea corymbosa – see an earlier section regarding this plant – and this was definitely employed for its hallucinogenic properties.

R. longeracemosa is a climbing vine with yellow flowers and beans mottled light and dark brown, while the species *R. pyramidalis* has greenish flowers and curious half-red and half-black seeds. These particular beans remind one of the oriental yin-yang symbol for chi energy and are actually used as good luck charms. The seeds of the species *phaseoloides* are very similar.

The vines grow in other tropical and semi-tropical countries of both hemispheres of the planet and bear their flowers in long racemes, similar to the flowering methods of other plants from the bean families. The leaves are actually quite similar to those of the edible runner bean.

Although an alkaloid similar to curare has been found in one species and an extract from *R. phaseoloides* was shown to produce a semi-torpor in a type of frog, far more extensive chemical testing and research is needed on these plants.

Puffballs
Lycoperdon marginatum, L. mixtecorum
Lycoperdaceae
Other common names: Gi 'I Wa, Gi 'I Sawa, Kalamoto

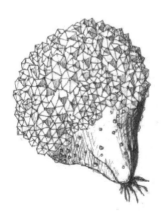

Lycoperdon Puffball (Illustration: Aziz Ipsule)

Puffballs is the name given to a group of unusual and unmistakable fungi from around the world. Some are small and some are very large, like the giant puffball (*Calvatia gigantea*), found in Europe and other parts of the northern hemisphere. There are several genera: *Lycoperdon, Bovista* and *Calvatia* being the main ones, but all are characterised by their more-or-less globular appearance and ability to discharge vast numbers of powdery spores, hence the common name.

Many beliefs in folklore have grown up around these strange fungi, for example, the Blackfoot Indian tribe call puffballs 'fallen stars', indicating where they believe the fungi originate. This tribe also burn puffballs as incense to repel ghosts.

Many species are edible when young, before they become full of powder-like spores. As with all fungi, though, it is most important to be able to identify such species beyond any shadow of doubt.

In this book, we are looking at psychoactive plant-life and amongst the puffballs we have a couple of candidates for this quality. In Mexico there appears to be at least three species that have been used this way or for magical purposes. The Tarahumara sorcerers of northern Mexico, it is reported by Schultes, Hofmann and other authors, use a species of *Lycoperdon* known as 'Kalamoto' to give themselves a cloak of invisibility for when they wish to approach a victim without being detected and also to make people ill. The Mixtec from the south of the country identify the species named after them (*L. mixtecorum*) by a descriptive appellation: 'gi 'i wa' meaning 'a fungus of the first quality'. It is said that this species has a sedative or hypnotic effect, which puts the consumer into a trance state in which auditory hallucinations such as voices or echoes are experienced. The Indians state that these voices will answer questions so this type of puffball, like the magic mushroom and the peyote cactus, which also speak, can be used to foretell events or as an oracle for divination. *L. mixtecorum* is a small species, just over 1in. across and only found in the region of Oaxaca. The other species they use is *L. marginatum* but this one is called 'gi 'i sawa' meaning 'fungus of second qualities', suggesting a less potent variety. *L. marginatum* also grows in Oaxaca and both species are found in pastures, grassy places and sparse woodland. The fungi are eaten to bring on their effects but there are no known substances identified from these puffballs that are recognised as intoxicants or hallucinogens.

There are probably other types of puffball with psychoactive properties and author Richard Rudgley, in his *The Encyclopedia of Psychoactive Substances*, informs readers about researcher and author Adrian Morgan's experiences. Morgan reported that only 15 minutes after eating just half an earthball *(Scleroderma citrina)* he experienced a 'strong narcosis' and 'visual disturbance giving way to a deep sleep lasting 2 hours'. The earthballs are similar in many ways to puffballs so it is perhaps not surprising if they are found to have effects that are the same or very alike.

S

Saguaro
Carnegia gigantea
Cactaceae

The saguaro is a very tall branching cactus, the kind associated with Western films in scenes of the prairie or desert. It actually reaches some 40ft. in height and is reputedly the largest of the columnar cacti. Even the branches can reach as much as 1–2½ foot in diameter. It is found growing in Mexico as well as many of the hot drier parts of both North and South America. The saguaro bears white funnel-shaped flowers at the top of its branches and these flowers are up to 5in. in length. They are followed by red or purplish oval-shaped berries, which contain many small black shiny seeds, so typical of many cactus species.

The saguaro cactus is utilised by many American Indian tribes for its medicinal purposes, for example, the Seri employ it as a remedy for rheumatism. The berries are valued as a food and also for wine-making.

Although this cactus adds much to the magical appearance of the traditional Western desert, there is little evidence of it being used in actual magical or shamanic ceremonies as an entheogen. Saguaro, it has been discovered, has the potential for this, however, as it contains carnegine, 5-hydroxycarnegine, norcarnegine and traces of 3-methoxytyramine and arizonine. These alkaloids have the capability of being psychoactive.

Salvia
Salvia divinorum, S. splendens
Lamiaceae
Other common names: Diviner's Mint, Diviner's Sage, Hierba de la Pastora (Herb of the Sheperdess), Hierba de la Virgen (Herb of the Virgin), Pipiltzintzintli, Ska Maria Pastora (all former names apply to *S. divinorum*), *Scarlet Sage, Splendid Salvia* (*S. splendens*)

Salvia Divinorum (Photo: Iolo Jones)

Salvia divinorum, a herb known and used for so long by Mazatec Indians of Oaxaca, Mexico, that as a possible 'cultigen' its original home and ancestry is unknown, is becoming one of the most widely sought after, cultivated, discussed and used entheogens in the world. Indeed, there have been websites with a large proportion of their content given over to the plant, an emailing list devoted to it, as well as books and other publications all about it. The herb has been on sale as dried foliage, as cuttings and rooted plants, and has been specially cultivated to supply the ever-growing demand, however, it has been made illegal, to varying degrees, in many parts of the world over the past decade (check the legal status of the plant where you are). So, what is so special about the diviner's mint to make it the focus of so much attention? Is it really so different from other hallucinogens and intoxicating herbs to deserve all this?

S. divinorum is a perennial plant in the sage genus, part of the huge family of mainly aromatic herbs the *Lamiaceae*, which has given us so many culinary, medicinal and psychoactive herbs, for example, thyme, mint, rosemary, motherwort and skullcap. But it really is something of an oddity on several counts.

First of all, is the question of where it actually originated from. The diviner's mint, unlike most of its cousins, is notoriously infertile and very seldom sets seed. In fact, it is probably safe to call it a self-sterile hybrid and plants grown from seed have been very rarely recorded. However, one documented case occurred in 1994 when it did produce seed. Daniel Siebert discovered seeds on the Wasson/Hofmann clone of the plant growing in Botanical Dimensions – a Botanical Gardens in Hawaii – and this represents the first documented instance of this. Pictures of the seeds and much more information is to be found in Daniel's salvia website: http://www.sagewisdom.org/

The fact that it generally proves infertile suggests that it is a 'cultigen' artificially and selectively bred and developed by human beings. As a matter of some significance and similarity, the *Brugmansia* species from South America, all of which are entheogens and used by the native shamans, also fall into this category, although these plants do set seed readily. If we accept that these plants do not grow naturally in the wild any more and that their true ancestry is unknown, we can only assume that they were selectively bred and cultivated for their psychoactive and other properties by some ancient culture or cultures of ancient American Indians. On a slightly fanciful note, it is even possible that they originated on the lost continent of Atlantis and maybe this is why we are so lacking in botanical history of these species? What is known is that the Mazatec Indians of Oaxaca cultivate the herb in plots in the damp forests there in the North-eastern Sierra Madre mountains. Also, that almost all the current crop of the herb being grown and distributed is, in fact, made up of clones of plants obtained from these people many years back by those famed ethnobotanists Hofmann and Wasson. Possibly, other tribes also cultivate and utilise the plant and this seems likely. According to the Salvia divinorum FAQ (part of Siebert's site) it is grown and used by the neighbouring tribes the Cuicatecs and Chinantecs. It is also considered very likely that the diviner's mint is the sacred herb known to the Aztecs as pipiltzintzintli.

Diviner's mint grows to 3ft. or more, sometimes reaching as much as 6ft. bearing 6in. long ovate leaves toothed along their edges. The flowers are bluish-white with small purplish sepals and are carried in long terminal panicles in the autumn. If the plant becomes top-heavy and falls over, it will send down adventitious roots at the nodes and start growing again from where it has fallen. It is a perennial but is sensitive to both frost and drought. It likes a damp, shady location with high humidity and a rich soil. It can be hardened off over a period of time but in such plants growth is very slow. Conversely, at a high temperature growth will be quickened but the air must be kept humid or the plant will suffer considerably.

The second reason that *S. divinorum* can be put in a class of its own is that the psychoactive substance it contains and the way this acts is unlike any other hallucinogenic alkaloid and so cannot be compared. In fact, it produces no effect at all at brain-cell receptor sites, normally showing chemical activity in tests. The active principle has been called 'Salvinorin A' and was first discovered in 1982 by Alfredo Ortega. Leander Valdes and others also isolated this substance a short while after this and were, at the time, unaware of Ortega's achievement. Valdes dubbed this psychoactive principle 'divinorum A' but the name got revised to Ortega's original after this was discovered. Salvinorin A is believed to be the most potent naturally occurring hallucinogenic substance known to science with doses of 100mcg producing noticeable effects and full effects at 1,000mcg. Daniel Siebert, who has widely publicised the plant's entheogenic properties, found as much as 0.44% of salvinorum A in the leaves, but average amounts of between 0.15% and 0.2% are more common. Salvinorin A is classed as a neo-clerodane diterpenoid and many species of salvia contain other neo-clerodanes or diterpenes, which are potentially psychoactive. Examples of such substances are 'salviarin', a new neo-clerodane from S. *splendens* and 'splendidin', a new trans-clerodane from the same species.

Salvinorin A has to be absorbed through the mucous membranes of the mouth, nose, lungs or anus in order to have an effect. If the herb or a preparation from it has been swallowed, the Salvinorin A is deactivated by the gastric secretions of the stomach, although if it can get into the intestines then it can be absorbed there. Generally speaking, eating or drinking salvia will not have much of an effect on many people. That being said, a traditional Mazatec shaman's method for administering the sacred herb is in a water-based drink but the reason this may work is due to the large amount of leaves used. There are 3 main ways of ingesting the active ingredient of this herb: the first and less damaging to the body is by chewing and holding a quid made up of fresh or dried leaves in the mouth. Between 8 and 16 large leaves is a dose but the Mazatec are known to use 13 pairs to make a quid. The quid, slowly chewed and then held in the mouth should start to take effect within 10–20 minutes and the resulting trip lasts about an hour. The second method is by smoking it, ideally through a water-pipe, because the smoke needs to be very hot to activate the salvinorin A and inhaled without some means of cooling it could easily cause damage to the lungs. One or two large leaves should produce a noticeable effect but the amounts needed may well vary with different individuals. The third and most powerful method is by vaporisation, which calls for heating the herb or extract to a high temperature, but not high enough to ignite it, and then inhaling the vapours given off. The herb could be vaporized using aluminium foil to hold it or a home-made apparatus could be constructed along the lines of those used for cannabis or opium. This method is the most dangerous, however, because the pure salvinorin A is rendered into a gaseous form and instantly absorbed. It can cause a state of total disassociation and loss of control and can even cause the person taking it to pass out. Clearly this could lead to a fire being started or other life-threatening complications and this method is to be approached with great caution and preferably with a trustworthy sitter on hand to deal with any emergency. Many neo-shamans, who have tried the herb in any or all of these ways, report an experience unlike other psychedelics or drugs.

So what are the hallucinogenic and psychoactive properties of the diviner's mint and what makes it so special? The Salvia divinorum FAQ gives an excellent 'trip rating scale' using the mnemonic S-A-L-V-I-A to indicate the 6 different levels of experience that may occur:

Level 1: 'S stands for stoning'. This means a mild marijuana type high.
Level 2: 'A stands for Altered Thought Processes'. At this level illogical thought patterns occur and short-term memory is impeded.
Level 3: 'L stands for LSD-like'. Anyone who has taken 'acid' or a strong hallucinogen would be familiar with this level. 'Eidetic' visual imagery is seen with the eyes closed, for example, geometric designs, fractals and cartoon imagery constantly changing form. With the eyes open things take on an animate quality with the feeling that walls and ceiling are moving, breathing and suchlike.
Level 4: 'V stands for Voyaging'. At this stage of the intoxication contact with spirits and other entities may occur together with visions of these beings and glimpses of other worlds and dimensions. This is the other world of

the experienced shaman.

Level 5: 'I stands for Identity Loss'. Here we reach the level of ego-loss and classic transcendental experience with a merging with everyone and everything, ideas of enlightenment and becoming at one with God/Goddess. Possibly a terrifying or ecstatic experience for the person on salvinorin A, but the observer may only witness a state of complete disorientation exhibited by the user.

Level 6: 'A stands for anaesthesia'. At this final level available, consciousness is lost. A person may fall, have seizures, remain immobile or behave in a manner like sleepwalking. Sensitivity to pain is also lost at this stage. On coming out of this state, no recollection of what was done or experienced or said will be available to the individual under the influence of salvinorin A. Obviously this last stage could be very dangerous if there is no one else present.

Possibly the best means of explaining the herb's effects is to give an account of one person's experience of using *S. divinorum* and below there follows such a report that I have very kindly been given permission to reproduce in full. This account also appeared in the Salvia divinorum FAQ. Greendrag had this to say about the experience:

A New Awareness through Salvia

The Setting:

A deserted beach in southern Mississippi on a bright, windy day. I was with my friend (let's call him M). He would be the trip sitter.

The Experience:

I sat down in a comfortable position with my head propped up and my hands folded. M filled the pipe (a cheap cannabis pipe) to the brim with Salvia. I found myself a bit nervous

... the same feeling one would feel before a carnival ride he/ she has never been on. M then lit the pipe and administered the first hit to me. I held it in for a good 20 seconds. Nothing much of a cannabis buzz happened for the first three hits. I signaled for a fourth hit. I held that in for a while, and then laid my head back. All of a sudden I fell into an amnesiac dream. I was thinking to myself ... that's weird nothing happened. That's it? That's what Salvia is like? I don't feel a thing! Wait a minute. I'm dreaming, but I'm not asleep! Here's how I described it to a friend:

'Imagine you are on this futuristic roller-coaster right before it takes off. You hear a voice that says "Get ready ... you are about to be catapulted off into the ride of your life" and then BANG ... you have no idea what just happened. You seemed to have dozed off right after the bang, but you're not sleeping. You then think to yourself am I in an amusement park? Wait, I went on the roller-coaster and I heard this voice tell me I am about to be catapulted into the ride of my life, or something. I don't remember anything after hearing that voice. Is THIS it??? It can't be ... it seems ... so familiar. Normal. I've done this a thousand times before I was old enough to retain memories. Wait ... is that ... I'm sleeping ... who is that ... this is so simple ... I understand perfectly ... things are always the same ...'

After smoking Salvia, I felt some sort of amnesia. I was not quite sure what happened after the third or fourth hit. I then realised something ... this WAS the trip. It was like I fell asleep for 10 years after the third hit, then right before I woke up, time travelled back 10 years and I woke up immediately after taking that hit.

During the moments after, I felt like I had done this a hundred times before. I felt like I was in a scene from my childhood ... almost as if I had smoked Salvia as a child and was feeling something in the present. I felt (note, I didn't see any of this, it was purely a feeling) like I was 8 years old, in a park around my house on a swing during the middle of a summer day. After I got this feeling, the feeling of the park transformed into where I was – the beach at present age. I then began to see (through closed eyelids) what looked like a ranch in Mexico. I then 'felt' that I was in the desert southwest, looking into this ranch. Through closed eyelids, I saw the beach I was on, but then a few yards away, the beach sand ended and the ranch/desert began. In the ranch I thought I saw a beautiful Mexican lady, but I could be wrong. I then felt I was on an Indian reservation with some Indians. I felt the feeling of the 'peyoteros'. I then felt the ranch/desert/ reservation drift away, not in a normal fashion, but in a 360 degree turn around my body. I then felt a closeness with the aura of it all. I got the feeling that Salvia was just one of a whole library of psychedelics just waiting to be used. I then felt 'normal' again and lay there still for a few moments, with my eyes closed. M had wandered off and I heard him in the distance. I then heard footsteps come behind the umbrellas, and then around them. I felt the presence of some old, yet beautiful man (could have been a woman) sprinkle some dust on me. I didn't feel the dust, but I felt something mentally. I then opened my eyes. If you have seen the movie 'Contact', I felt exactly like what happened to Jodie Foster as she crashed onto the beach after being transported in that machine. Also, the scene afterward where she comes back to Earth, yet still feeling she was on that beach. BTW, this was about 5–10 minutes after I had smoked that last hit.

I sat up and walked off to the edge of the beach. I was left with a sort of knowingness. I realised many things at this point after the experience. I would call THIS the best part of the trip. The theories I had come up with days before seemed to make sense. EVERYTHING seemed to make total sense. I thought about the world I live in. That didn't make sense.

Commercialism, money, business, finance, government ... that made no sense. I realised that things such as fear (such as that of ghosts), jealousy, anxiety, stress, fright ... these were things that are human. These things are built into the human mind to act as hurdles that we must jump. She said that things such as fundamentalist religion and science were parts of this 'human' quality. None of these 'human' things made sense. I realised that in the afterworld (or whatever), these things are no longer present. The human brain acts as a filter for our soul. We cannot directly experience the things our soul feels, so it gets filtered through our brain. This filter adds things such as fear and hate to the things that our soul feels. I felt like that filter had been removed for a while. This I repeated to myself, 'If only they knew.' I had the feeling of having gone to Heaven. I was also shown the goodness of psychedelic drugs. She told me that she had many, many 'friends' ... many of them haven't been discovered yet. I walked back to the umbrellas to M. He asked me how it was. I just sat there silent, meditative. I told him, 'I can't tell you what this is.' I had no sense of shock. I had no sense of WOW, no sense of surprise. It was just a sense of knowingness, understanding, calmness, peace. I remained silent for the whole 'afterglow' period. Now, I look at things a different way. Salvia is definitely a 'teacher' plant. I now look upon her (and her friends) very seriously and in the utmost respect.

So, there you have one person's account of the Salvia experience and contact with a plant 'teacher', felt in this case to be probably female. Make of it what you will but remember that the diviner's mint can transport the user out of this world for a while and that in a disoriented state it is possible to have a nasty accident. Therefore, the caution is repeated to always have a sitter present if intending to ingest this powerful plant.

The Mazatec shamans, besides employing the herb for

mystical and divinatory purposes also use it to treat illnesses such as colds, sore throats, constipation and diarrhoea, as well as conditions originating within the psyche. However, all of these ailments and their causes would be viewed within the framework of their belief system, which takes into account the influence of spirits and other worldly influences.

Salvia splendens (Photo: Iolo Jones)

Besides *S. divinorum*, its close relative *S. splendens* is causing a lot of discussion too, due to the psychoactive effects it is reported to have. This species is commonly grown in gardens and parks throughout the world as an attractive border plant. It is commonly known as the scarlet sage and will grow as a perennial to several feet in height. Usually it is thought of as a summer bedding flower and treated as an annual, but in both cases either as a short-lived summer bedding plant or as a longer-lived perennial, it produces toothed dark-green foliage and terminal racemes of bright red or scarlet flowers and bracts. There are many cultivated varieties with descriptive names like Blaze of Fire and Rose Flame and some of these are dwarf in habit.

According to reports, the action of this herb, if taken in the same way as *S. divinorum*, produces a very different noticeable effect, which is described as a state of strong relaxation and serenity. The effects have also been said to resemble those caused by a benzodiazepine tranquilizer like Valium, but with a mental clarity retained, and also akin to an opiate-induced sensation. Many people report that it causes a form of 'don't care either way' acceptance of things. Splendidin and salviarin, the active constituents have been described as anxiolytic in their action but possibly superior in their effects to the usual tranquilizers which can dull perceptions and confuse thought. The herb is also said to enhance sexual pleasure. Because *S. splendens* is a comparatively new species of herb to be experimented with as an entheogen its potential for adverse reactions and toxic effects are, as yet, not very well known or documented. It is claimed to work synergistically when mixed with its cousin *S. divinorum* and often the two herbs have been sold as mixed batches of foliage by dealers.

The common cooking sage *S. officinalis* contains thujone in very small quantities, which is psychoactive and also is said to cause potential brain damage when too much is taken. This substance is also found in wormwood (*Artemesia spp.*) and, along with alcohol, gives an intoxicating effect to absinthe. Juniper (*Juniperus communis*) contains thujone as well, and has been found to be psychoactive when smoked.

An unidentified *Salvia*, known as 'Xiwit' to the Nahuatl tribe of Sierra de Puebla in Mexico has been reported to be used to induce dreams. Nothing much else is known about it except that it is not *S. divinorum*.

According to one of the world's best-known herbalists Nicholas Culpeper, the common sage is ruled by Jupiter, but he also informs us, when describing the wood sage (*Teucrium scorodonia*) that, 'The Sages are under Venus.' We may make of this what we will when trying to ascertain planetary rulers for the diviner's mint and the scarlet sage.

Scirpus
Scirpus atrovirens
Cyperaceae
Other common names: Bakana, Bakanawa, Bakanoa

Scirpus (Illustration: Aziz Ipsule)

Scirpus is the generic name for grass-like plants from the sedge family. In Mexico, the Tarahumara use an unidentified species that they call 'bakana' as a hallucinogen for shamanic usage and also to treat illnesses in the tribe. Although the actual species is unknown for certain, Schultes and Hofmann chose the species *atrovirens* to be named and illustrated. Some species from the genus and related sedges are known to contain harmala ß-carboline alkaloids, which have hallucinatory effects, although whether these are the active substances in the plant known as 'bakana' remains to be discovered. Whatever species it is, it is associated with insanity, both as a cure for mental instability and as a herb of protection for those who suffer in this way. At the same time, it is reported that the Indians fear to cultivate the plant lest they go mad. If the herb is a powerful hallucinogen, then such a natural respect for the plant might be prudent and not some strange belief based on nothing more than mumbo-jumbo.

It is stated that the tubers of the plant are the parts that produce the psychoactive effects. These include transporting the spirit of the user to distant locations (sounds like what is commonly known in occultism as astral travel), enabling communication with the dead, causing a deep sleep and producing vivid and brightly-coloured hallucinations. Apparently, the Indians must perform rituals to the herb, showing great respect and even offering food to the deities that preside over the plants. Special songs are also sung to appease the spirits of the herb.

Some types of *Scirpus* are annuals and others are perennial, but most species seem to prefer to grow in damp and boggy areas. The genus *Scirpus* is cosmopolitan in its distribution.

Screw-Pine
Pandanus odoratissimus, Pandanus spp.
Pandanaceae

Various species of screw-pine have been reported to have been used by the Chimbu people of New Guinea for hallucinogenic purposes but details are sketchy, save that it is known that the fruit is the part consumed. Dimethyltryptamine (DMT) has been extracted from the nuts and as this is a potent hallucinogen, this is the likely culprit behind outbreaks of 'irrational behaviour' known as 'Karuka madness'. This is said to occur after the natives have consumed large quantities of the nuts of the screw-pine.

The screw-pine is a very large tree-like or shrubby plant given to a climbing nature, often bearing long stilt-like roots hanging down and propping the plant up. The leaves are very vicious looking, growing as stiff swords to a length of up to 15ft. These leaves are also armed with prickles that are hooked both backwards and forwards. Despite their dangers these leaves are often used as fibrous matting. The large flower-heads are enclosed in spathes and after flowering, a hard cone-like aggregate fruit is formed. This is almost globular in shape and contains the nuts.

The screw-pine grows along coasts and in salt-marshes.

Senecio
Senecio cardiophyllus, S. cervariaefolius, S. grayanus, S. hartwegii, S. jacobaea, S. praecox, S. toluccanus
Asteraceae
Other common names: Ragwort, Palo bobo, Palo loco, Quantlapatziinzintli

Various species of the genus *Senecio* from the family *Compositae* have been reported as being used for their psychoactive properties by the Mexican Indians and to be included in their

Senecio jacobaea (Photo: Tim Brett)

medicinal herbs as well. Over 60 different species grow in Mexico and there is some doubt over exactly which species are the ones in use. *S. praecox* has golden-yellow ray flowers so typical of the genus. It grows to the size of a small tree or large shrub, reaching a maximum of 15ft. and has been employed as a remedy for rheumatism and wounds. The herb is also said to 'produce delusions'.

The genus *Senecio* has a cosmopolitan distribution over the planet and occurs in the form of annuals, biennials, short-lived perennials and also as woody climbing perennials or shrubs. Most of the plants in this genus are considered toxic to a degree and alkaloids contained in them may be injurious to the liver. The European ragwort *S. jacobaea*, which has spread to many other parts of the world, including Australia, is believed to be one of the most sacred herbs of the fairy folk and in some Celtic countries, like Ireland, it was considered bad luck to destroy the plant. Its poisonous properties are taken onboard by the caterpillars of the cinnabar moth (*Tyria jacobaeae*) and both the larvae and the adult moths wear warning colours to inform predators of their toxic nature. The caterpillars are brightly banded in orange and black and the attractive adult moths, which often fly by day and are mistaken for butterflies, are arrayed in black and red.

A tea is prepared from the leaves of *Senecio spp.* for herbal medicinal uses and as an intoxicant. The plant is known to contain toxic pyrrolizidine alkaloids and is not recommended for domestic use because it is dangerous.

The herbs of the genus *Senecio* are governed astrologically by the planet Venus.

Sida
Sida acuta, S. rhombifolia
Malvaceae
Other common names: Axocatzin, Common Sida, Chichipe, Malva colorada

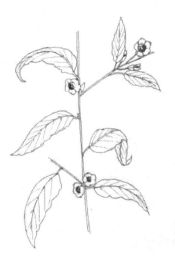

Sida (Illustration: Aziz Ipsule)

S

Sida is the generic name for two shrubby evergreen plants, which can reach as much as 9ft. in height and come from Asia. This herb is also found growing in many semi-tropical and tropical countries including Mexico and Central America as well as some parts of Australia. The flowers are usually yellow but can be white and are borne in the leaf axils. The plant is a vigorous grower but likes a light well-drained soil in a sunny position. It is drought and frost sensitive. Sida can be propagated by seed or cuttings.

Sida is unusual in being a psychoactive member of the mallow family, a family, which although it has many medicinal and culinary herbs, has few that cause effects to the mind. Its leaves are commonly smoked in many countries, especially Mexico, for their euphoric and stimulating effects. In India a tea is made, which has the same qualities and, when chilled, is an excellent and cooling beverage for hot and clammy weather. According to Torsten Wiedemann of Shaman Australis Botanicals a tea brewed from about 10–20g of root also has a stimulating effect.

The shrub owes its properties to pseudoephedrine and/or ephedrine, as well as ß-phenethylamine. It also contains vascin, choline and hipaphorine. Sida is used medicinally by the Australian Aborigines as a remedy for diarrhoea amongst other ailments.

Sinicuichi
Heimia salicifolia
Lythraceae
Other common names: Abre-o-sol ('Sun Opener'), Herba da Vida ('Herb of Life'), Plant of Yellow Vision

Sinicuichi is a herb from the loosestrife family, currently the subject of much research in academic and ethnobotanical circles. It grows to as much as 6ft. in height and is found from Mexico to Argentina. Like many members of this family it prefers to grow

Heimia salicifolia (Photo: Tim Brett)

in moist places such as along the sides of streams and rivers and also in mountainous areas. It is fairly hardy but doesn't tolerate drought well or solid freezes. It bears thin lanceolate leaves similar to those of the willow, hence its botanical name and small single yellow flowers in the leaf-axils along the uppermost parts of the stems. The persistent and bell-shaped calyx, which houses the flower, develops long appendages like horns. It can become quite shrubby with woody stems but the overall appearance of the herb is a delicate and dainty plant. There are two other similar species in the genus which play an extensive role in folk-medicine of the Central and South American Indians but only the species *salicifolia* appears to exhibit psychoactive qualities and to have been used accordingly.

In Mexico the leaves of the plant are collected, allowed to wilt and then crushed in water and left to ferment into an intoxicating beverage. This drink is said to cause a giddy feeling, a darkening of what is perceived, a pleasant drowsiness with possible memories from long, long ago recalled, and auditory hallucinations of voices and sounds becoming distorted so they appear to come from far away. It is reported that Aztec

S

and Mexican Indian shamans have used the plant as a trance divinatory herb. There are, however, some authorities, which claim that it has none of these effects.

Heimia salicifolia contains the alkaloids cryogenine (vertine), lyfoline, lythrine, nesodine and others of a quinolizidine type, as well as other minor alkaloids. A new alkaloid called heimidine has also been identified. According to an ethnopharmacological report prepared by M. H. Malone and A. Rother of the Department of Physiology and Pharmacology, of the University of the Pacific, Stockton, California, USA, *Heimia salicifolia* has 'a reputation as an antisyphilitic, sudorific, antipyretic, laxative and diuretic'. The report goes on to state that it could also be used to prepare post-partum baths and to help heal wounds. Some research has indicated that the herb has an anti-inflammatory and analgesic effect similar to aspirin and this is of interest when we consider that aspirin comes from the willow (*Salix species*), which *Heimia* resembles in other ways, as already noted.

Solandra
Solandra brevicalyx, S. guerrerensis, S. maxima
Solanaceae
Other common names: Chalice Vine, Golden Cup Vine, Kieli, Hueipatl, Tecomaxochitl

The various species of *Solandra* are shrubs or climbers and produce showy flowers, similar to those of their relatives the *brugmansias*, which are in the same family. The flowers are cream or yellow in colour and likened to a funnel or a chalice in shape. They are strongly scented and can reach as much as 10in. in length. Like the *brugmansia* species, these plants also contain various potent tropane alkaloids, which besides being very toxic and to be approached with much caution, also are capable of producing very strong hallucinatory effects and delusional states. *Solandra* species have leathery leaves and are

Solandra (Illustration: Aziz Ipsule)

semi-evergreen but tender and need a warm temperature. Many types are grown as ornamentals for the sheltered spot or the greenhouse.

In Mexico, the Indian shamans of some tribes make a tea from the sap of the branches of *S. brevicalyx* and *S. guerrerensis*, the latter of which takes its name from the State of Guerrero, where it grows and is used as an intoxicant. It is reported that Hernández stated that the Aztecs knew the plant as 'Tecomaxochitl' or 'Hueipatl'. The two species of *Solandra* described here are known to have played a large part in the folklore and belief system of the Huichol Indians and presumably of other tribes as well.

Like many of the dangerous but potent hallucinogens in the *Solanaceae* the herbs of the genus *Solandra* contain the tropanes scopolamine and hyoscyamine, together with some lesser-known alkaloids such as nortropine, tropine and cuscohygrine.

T

Tagetes
Tagetes lucida, T. minuta
Asteraceae

Other common names: Pericón, Sweet-scented Marigold, Tarragon, Tumutsali, Yahutli, Yia, Xpuhuc

Tagetes (Photo: Iolo Jones)

Tagetes species are often grown in gardens as attractive border plants and these types are known as African, American, Aztec and French marigolds. They come in many different colours and forms with double-flowered and dwarf varieties. They are treated as annuals, although many species are actually perennial by nature. The species that concern us here, however, are found in the wild in Mexico and other parts of Central and South America. *Tagetes lucida* is very common in the Mexican states of Nayarit and Jalisco. This species grows to about 1½ foot with branching stems and very aromatic dark-green leaves, serrated at the edges. The flowers are fairly small and golden or orange-yellow in colour and are carried in terminal clusters from summer to autumn.

The Indians of the Sierra Madre have a cultural tradition of smoking *T. lucida* for recreational purposes, and the Huichol tribe mix the herb with tobacco (*Nicotiana rustica*) in the hope of producing visions. As well as this, the tribe often drinks a fermented brew of maize known as 'Cai' or 'Tesguino' and this is reported 'to produce clearer visions'. The Zapotec Indians employ *T. lucida* in purification rituals and the ancient Mayans are said to have used it as a trance 'tobacco'. According to Torsten Wiedemann and others, the Aztecs used the herb for serious ceremonies and rituals, including administering enough of the powdered plant to numb their victims before sacrificing them in fire rituals to their gods. The herb when smoked is said to produce 'closed-eye images' as spectacular as those of peyote, although no strong hallucinogenic alkaloids have been isolated from the plant.

T. lucida is used medicinally in Mexico to treat many ailments including rheumatism and stomach troubles. It is said to aid lactation too. The plant has a strong chocolate liquorice or aniseed taste and is popular as a culinary herb to add a distinctive flavouring to soups, meat and vegetable dishes.

The related *T. minuta* is reportedly even stronger in psychoactive properties and is considered a preferred strain of marigold by many who like to indulge.

It is of interest to note that the *Tagetes* species have insect and pest-repellent properties too and can be used to drive away mosquitoes amongst other nuisance tiny creatures. Gardeners can employ these herbs to battle against nematode worms and pests like aphids and whitefly. Even growing a specimen of *Tagetes* alongside another plant is thought to offer it some protection. Recent studies have shown anti-viral properties too.

The whole genus is rich in essential oils, as well as coumarin and thiophene derivatives and saponines, tannins and cyanogenic glycosides have also been reported.

Teonanacatl

Conocybe siligineoides, Panaeolus campanulatus, Paneolus/ Paneolina foenisecii, Panaeolus sphinctrinus, Psilocybe acutissima, Psilocybe aztecorum, Psilocybe caerulescens, Psilocybe caerulescens var. albida, Psilocybe caerulescens var. mazatecorum, Psilocybe caerulescens var. nigripes, Psilocybe caerulipes, Psilocybe cordispora, Psilocybe fagicola, Psilocybe hoogshagenii, Psilocybe isauri, Psilocybe mexicana, Psilocybe mixaeensis, Psilocybe muliercula, Psilocybe semperviva, Psilocybe wassonii (Syn. P. wassoniorum), Psilocybe yungensis, Psilocybe zapotecorum, Stropharia cubensis (Syn. P. cubensis) **Agaricaceae, Coprinaceae, Strophariaceae**

Other common names: The Aztecs called sacred mushrooms 'Teonanacatl'. Various other names have been given to the different species and by different tribes. The Mazatec and Chinatec refer to *P. sphinctrinus* as 'Ta-ha-na-sa, To-shka' ('Intoxicating mushroom') and 'She-to' ('Pasture mushrooms'). The Mazatec Indians call *S. cubensis* 'Di-shi-tjo-le-rra-ja' ('Divine Mushroom of Manure') while in Oaxaca it is known as 'Hongo de San Isidro'.

Psilocybe hoogshagenii (Illustration: Aziz Ipsule)

I have grouped all the 'sacred' or 'magic mushrooms' of Mexico under the one name used by the Aztecs. This is done for convenience because there are so many species used by so many different tribes that it all can get very confusing, to say the least. The one thing that is common to them all is that they contain psilocybin and psilocin, which are very potent and well-known hallucinogenic substances. Incidentally, 'teonanacatl' means 'God's flesh', which indicates the very high regard that has been held for these fungi. Apparently, the sixteenth-century Franciscan missionary Bernardino de Sahagún, writing in the *General History of the Things of New Spain* stated that the Aztecs used this term for a sacred mushroom. However, although he made it clear that it was a fungus, which was referred to, this was subsequently challenged by the idea that teonanacatl was actually the peyote cactus. Richard Schultes, early in his career as an ethnobotanist, agreed with the Franciscan monk and then when travelling in Mexico discovered that the Mazatec, Chinantec and Zapotec tribes of the Oaxaca area made use of various species of *Paneolus* for their psychoactive properties. He assumed that this was the genus of fungus that teonanacatl referred to. Some time after this, he found out that the Indians also consumed various other types of fungus not in this genus and from this he realised that it was a general term for sacred mushroom. The difficulties a researcher runs into when trying to investigate the history of mushroom use among the tribes of Central America was compounded by efforts of the early Church fathers to demonise the practice and to eradicate the knowledge and use of the sacred mushrooms. They were not successful, however, because the Mexican Indian mushroom cults simply went underground or became disguised by mixing in the practice with elements of Christian worship. The practice of gathering the mushrooms and using them for shamanic purposes has continued on from that period and one of the main tribes to practise the use of teonanacatl in their ceremonies is the

T

Mazatec.

An interesting point is raised by controversial author David Icke in his work *The Biggest Secret*. Icke tells us that the early Essenes had a detailed knowledge of hallucinogenic herbs and regarded magic mushrooms as so sacred that they had a ritual for their gathering, which took place before sunrise. These fungi were held in such great respect that the Jewish priests of the time wore mushroom-shaped caps. Considering this information, I realised that the traditional shape for a synagogue is a dome, which might also be symbolic of a mushroom. Perhaps the house of the Lord is shaped like a mushroom cap?

Getting back to Mexican history, many centuries later on from the Essene brotherhood, it seems sadly ironic that the Church did all it could to stamp out the use of the very fungi regarded as 'God's flesh', by the Indians of the New World. These were the fungi that the early Essene priesthood held in such high esteem and as sacred mushrooms. It seems very likely that these early priests and their religious beliefs and writings formed a large part of what the modern Christian and Catholic churches were based upon.

But how were the mushrooms used and what effects did they create? Dr. Schultes wrote that the doses the Mazatec used varied with the age and size of the individual taking them but that usually 15 mushrooms were considered enough for an effect. He reported that the hallucinogenic and intoxicant properties of the mushrooms were felt shortly after ingestion when:

the subject experiences a general feeling of levity and well-being. This exhilaration is followed within an hour by hilarity, incoherent talking, uncontrolled emotional outbursts and, in the latter stages of intoxication, by fantastic visions in brilliant colours.

So, that is how Dr. Richard Schultes would describe the

psychoactive properties of psilocybin-containing mushrooms, and bearing this in mind, I thought that I would like to make a personal description of the potential effects that can be experienced:

As the mushrooms start to take effect there may be feelings of nausea and anxiety, thinking processes may get muddled slightly and a drowsy feeling may set in. You may yawn profusely. Along with this there may be some feelings of apprehension and edginess. It may be difficult to follow a conversation properly and a loss of the instinctive sense of passing of time may disappear. You may feel strangely out of sync with your companions. These negative feelings soon are displaced by a growing awareness that the psilocybin is starting to really 'kick in'. Colours become brighter and depth and dimension starts to get added to objects and textures around you. It may well appear that everything is moving or breathing. An alive quality is expressed by inanimate objects and living creatures and plants become so much more so as well as possibly expressing some new spiritual character. Patterns that were not there before start to form on surfaces. These patterns may be geometric or even like Celtic knot-work. A feeling of euphoria, friendliness and an increase in energy levels may be felt. A 'very stoned' feeling with a strong tendency to fits of uncontrollable laughter may erupt. Sometimes you know why you are laughing and other times you do not but are unable to stop. This may cause potentially embarrassing situations in social settings or you may feel that it doesn't matter what others think anyway! As the intoxication progresses all manner of philosophical insights may come to you. Perhaps you may realise that everything is actually alive and all things are part and parcel of some immense beingness. Perhaps you will feel that it is incredibly amusing that you are able to see and hear and experience all these things while everyone else cannot. The quality of sounds distorts so that background noise becomes louder or voices and other sounds may become difficult to comprehend. Music may become so much better or lose its usual appeal. You may experience inner voices or have the sensation that objects or living things like trees are able to communicate. The twigs and branches of trees may appear to move as if under a strobe light and this movement adds to the feeling of how alive they are. As well as all this, the environment you are in may take on the appearance and feel of another time or place or maybe even of another planet. Perhaps everything will seem like part of a sci-fi movie or you may get a sense of being in another age such as medieval times. Faces of people may change so much you cannot recognise them or they may exhibit a form of shape-shifting. This may be disconcerting until you realise that what is going on is the effect of the mushroom and make efforts to compensate. If you close your eyes all manner of complex scenarios are presented with visions of beautiful buildings in strange and exotic cities, ever-changing cartoons, fantastic coloured geometric patterns that like fractals lead further into more areas of wonder. The degree of artistry expressed and the complexity of these inner visions would outdo the greatest painter who has ever lived and yet these 'masterpieces' are being fashioned in split-second timing and replaced just as quickly. When you open your eyes and as the trip intensifies, all manner of geometric designs and symbols may appear to fill all the vacant space you are looking into. At higher levels of the experience it can become very similar to that brought about by LSD, although usually a lot gentler and with a far more organic feel. After reaching a peak, the whole visionary experience starts to subside in intensity and brings you back into the everyday world.

At low doses the experience lasts usually no more than from 2–4 hours but if larger quantities are ingested, the duration will be extended and made much more intense. It is wise to remember that psilocybin and psilocin are very potent mind-altering substances that can drastically alter the world you are experiencing. Like with 'acid' very unpleasant psychotic and paranoid reactions are possible. For this reason these mushrooms are to be treated with great respect and are not to be carelessly dabbled with. In many countries and states, the powers that be have classified the substances in these fungi as Class A drugs so this fact, too, should be remembered.

Over two dozen species are known as being employed as entheogens by the Mexican Indians and there are all manner of variations in the preferences of the shamans for one species over another and for the methods of using them. Often a natural crop of one species will turn out poor so another type would be substituted. One of the main favoured species is *Psilocybe mexicana* and it was from this type that Dr Albert Hofmann first isolated and named the active compounds psilocybin and psilocin. Hofmann worked with laboratory grown specimens but the fungus was officially 'rediscovered' by Roger Heim as late as 1956. It is a small and dainty mushroom with the cap usually between 1 and 2cm only. The stems are from 1–4in. high. The colour is a brownish-red or more commonly a yellowish shade like that of straw. Like many other species in this genus it has a nipple at the top. It dries to a greenish-tan or a dark yellow. When fresh it stains blue if bruised showing the presence of the hallucinogenic substances it contains. *P. mexicana* is found singly or in small groups in grassy areas on the edges of woods, in pastures and along the sides of roads and trails. It prefers a limestone based soil and likes to grow in mountainous areas at altitudes of 4500–5000ft. The fungus bears fruit from April through to October. It also grows in parts of Guatemala.

This was the species that Dr. Hofmann ingested in an effort to find out if artificially cultured specimens retained the properties of wild mushrooms. He took 32 mushrooms and his account published in *The Botany and Chemistry of Hallucinogens* is one of the most famous pioneering reports on the psychedelic experience. Here is his account of that 'trip':

As I was perfectly aware that my knowledge of the Mexican origin of the mushrooms would lead me to imagine only Mexican scenery, I tried deliberately to look on my environment as I knew it normally. But all voluntary efforts to look at things in their customary forms and colours proved ineffective. Whether my eyes were closed or open, I saw only Mexican motifs and colours. When the doctor supervising the experiment bent over me to check my blood pressure, he was transformed into an Aztec priest, and I would not have been astonished if he had drawn an obsidian knife. In spite of the seriousness of the situation, it amused me to see how the Germanic face of my colleague had acquired a purely Indian expression. At the peak of the intoxication, about 1½ hours after ingestion of the mushrooms, the rush of interior pictures, mostly changing in shape and colour, reached such an alarming degree that I feared I would be torn into this whirlpool of form and colour and would dissolve. After about 6 hours, the dream came to an end. Subjectively, I had no idea how long this condition had lasted. I felt my return to everyday reality to be a happy return from a strange, fantastic but quite really experienced world into an old and familiar home.

Another popular member of the fungi classed as teonanacatl is *Psilocybe hoogshagenii*, another species 'rediscovered' by Roger Heim and named as a mark of tribute to Searle Hoogshagen, who aided Wasson with his important research work in his 1954 expedition to Mexico. This species is very distinctive with a curiously curved and extended nipple at the top of the cap. It likes muddy clay-based soils and also has an affinity for coffee plantations. *P. hoogshagenii* is found in the Mexican states of Oaxaca, Puebla and Chiapas and is also reported from locations in South America including parts of Argentina and Colombia.

It is regarded by the Indian shamans as a particularly wise

mushroom spirit and is much sought after when decision making is called for in a ceremony or rite. The Mixe think of it as a 'Judge'.

Other *psilocybe* species that are found in Mexico and are reported as being used as teonanacatl are *P. acutissima, P. aztecorum, P. caerulescens, P. caerulipes, P. cordifolia, P. fagicola, P. isauri, P. mixaeensis, P. muliercula, P. semperviva, P. wassoniorum, P. yungensis* and *P. zapotecorum.*

In addition to the *psilocybe* mushrooms, fungi from the genus *Paneolus* have been also grouped in with the others as teonanacatl. In particular, the species *Paneolus campanulatus, P. sphinctrinus* and *P. foenisecii (Syn. Paneolina foenisecii)* are reported as mushrooms that may be used as hallucinogens. In fact, Mexican shamans of the Mazatec and Chinantec tribes are said to employ species of *Paneolus* in their rituals. These species of *Paneolus* mushroom are also widely distributed throughout many temperate areas of the globe including much of Europe; in fact, they could justifiably be classed as cosmopolitan. They like to grow in fields and grassy places and *sphinctrinus*, in particular, has an affinity for pastures where there is plenty of cow dung. It is about 4in. in height with a dull brown or greyish cap that is campanulate in shape and which attains over 1in. in diameter. *P. sphinctrinus* is easily recognisable because of a set of teeth forming a dainty frill around the edges of the caps. This species is commonly known as the 'Petticoat Fungus' and also as 'Grey Mottle Gill'. Although it has not been widely used as a hallucinogenic agent, it has been reported to have proved to be psychoactive. *P. foenisecii* is a very common and widely distributed species, often found growing in large numbers in lawns. It is commonly known as the Haymaker's mushroom and has been listed as containing psilocybin, although this has been found to be incorrect.

Author, website host, and very diligent mushroom researcher John Allen aka 'Mushroom John' has, with the help of Mark

D. Merlin, co-authored a very well argued and sourced article entitled *Observations Regarding the Suspected Psychoactive Properties of Paneolus Foenisecii Maire*. The authors take an in-depth look at the history of suspected poisonings and intoxications caused by this common fungus and conclude that it is actually non-psychoactive, save for a possible feeling of relaxation engendered by tryptamine alkaloids the fungus contains, including 5-hydroxytryptophan. The authors state that the amounts of the hallucinogenic substances in the mushroom are far too small to have any noticeable effect unless vast amounts were consumed. They point out that in reports of children supposedly affected by these mushrooms it was possible that other psychoactive plant material had been ingested. Also, that in studies of the amount of psilocybin and psilocin in this fungus, a batch collected for analysis may be contaminated by other similar but more potent species found growing in the same location. John has told me that, in addition, he disagrees with the opinions of Schultes, Hofmann et al. regarding the properties of *P. sphinctrinus* and that he can back up his claims in similar fashion. Full marks to a man who not only does an incredible amount of research but who is also not afraid of challenging the status quo!

One of the largest magic mushrooms found growing in Mexico and also throughout much of the semi-tropical and tropical areas of the globe is the well-known *Stropharia cubensis*, also known as *Psilocybe cubensis*. This mushroom is thought to have originated in Asia and been introduced along with cattle brought to America. It has a liking for fields with plenty of cattle dung and the Mazatec name for the fungus is Di-shi-tjo-le-rra-ja, meaning 'divine mushroom of manure'. The fungus can grow to as much as 5¾ inches in height but is usually about 3 inches and the tawny brown or tan semi-conical caps reach up to 2 inches across. Probably because it is not native to Mexico some Indian shamans, including the well-known Maria Sabina, have refused to use this species. Nevertheless, inspired by the mushrooms she does use, the shaman had this to say:

> The sacred mushroom takes me by the hand and brings me to the world where everything is known. It is they, the sacred mushrooms, that speak in a way I can understand. I ask them and they answer me. When I return from the trip that I have taken with them, I tell what they have told me and what they have shown me.

Stropharia cubensis (Illustration: Aziz Ipsule)

S. cubensis, however, is an excellent source of psilocybin and is very popular with many shamans and neo-shamans alike. It also lends itself well to cultivation on compost and is probably the most widely grown species of magic mushroom in the world, even though it is now illegal in many countries and states.

Finally, the *Conocybe* genus of mushrooms has also been reported as containing the psychoactive alkaloids psilocybin and psilocin and the species *C. siligineoides*, which grows in Mexico, is thought to be one of the many sacred intoxicating mushrooms used by the Indians and their shamans. It is found on rotten wood and grows to about 3in. high with a 1in. fawn or orange-red cap.

An organisation was set up in Canada called The Fane of the Psilocybe, which has tried to get legal rights to possess psilocybin mushrooms for ingestion as a religious sacrament. The members of the group believe that individuals should have the right to alter their perceptions by the use of entheogens for purposes of enlightenment and spiritual and inner-search. They are against the consumption of psilocybin mushrooms by the 'unprepared' and stress that the mushrooms are used as sacraments.

Toloache
Datura inoxia (innoxia), Datura inoxia(innoxia) spp. inoxia (innoxia), (Syn. D. meteloides)
Solanaceae
Other common names: Sacred Datura, Devil's Weed, Downy Thornapple, Toloatzin

Toloache is the name given to *Datura inoxia*, which is regarded as probably the most important and widely known Mexican representative of this dangerous but very potent genus of entheogens. All of the daturas contain the tropane alkaloids, atropine, hyoscine, scopolamine and hyoscyamine, which means that they are potentially very toxic but also very strong hallucinogens. Like their cousins the Brugmansias from South America, they are widely used for shamanic purposes, including initiatory rites, by many Native American tribes. These herbs also have traditional medicinal uses, as do their relatives, such as *D. stramonium*. In both mainstream and herbal medicines of the East and West, daturas are employed as treatments for asthma and for their anti-spasmodic, anodyne and narcotic properties. It should be stressed here that the use of this herb for medicinal properties should never be for domestic purposes but only under the guidance of an experienced medical practitioner.

Toloache is a perennial species growing to 3ft. or more with greyish leaves covered in fine hairs. It has funnel-shaped flowers typical of this genus and these can reach as much as 5½–9in. in length. These blooms are enticingly scented with an almost erotic perfume and are white tinged with pink or violet. The flowers are followed by the distinctive thornapples, which are prickly and can easily remind one of horse-chestnuts, as they are about the same size and covered in similar spines. Toloache grows in waste places and on arable land and besides Mexico is also to be encountered in the South-western parts of America as well as in various subtropical and tropical areas of the globe.

The sub-species *D. inoxia inoxia* is often referred to as the Sacred Datura and the Downy Thornapple. It has been a chosen herb for shamanic purposes for various tribes of the Southern states of North America, as well as for those of Central America, and the list of these tribal peoples includes the Navajo and the Zuni. The Yokut, another of the tribes that use it, take the seeds once in a lifetime as an initiation into manhood. This indicates just how potent a hallucinogen the herb is and also how very dangerous it can be. The hallucinations are extreme and often involve visions of beings known or unknown and the user is taken so far from the reality of his or her actual companions that he or she may feel convinced that he or she is in some entirely different location. The experience has the reality of a dream and the reality factor can be so convincing that the intoxicated person may even carry on conversations with beings they encounter and make use of items invisible to any witness who may be present. For example, someone on datura may believe they are with someone else who smokes and may start to pass invisible cigarettes or 'joints' to their invisible companion. For some unknown reason this delusion is often reported as part of the intoxication with this herb. This is the very stuff of madness and may well lead someone under its influence into the mental institution. The dangerous toxins in the plant may even lead to a fatal poisoning and the 'trip' would be the last one the would-be experimenter with toloache would take.

The species *inoxia* was one of the sacred power plants of the Aztecs but in more recent times has been used by the Tarahumara as an ingredient of an intoxicating maize drink known as 'tesquino'. The roots, seeds and leaves are all added to give the brew an extra kick and there is no doubt that they certainly make it a very strong drink indeed!

Nevertheless, it is reported that the Indians believe that Toloache is presided over by a malevolent plant spirit. All of the daturas are, as already pointed out, very dangerous plants to consume, so the Indian beliefs are rooted in scientific and medical fact. The tropanes contained in the herb cause some very unpleasant and life-threatening side effects, which include dry mouth, blurred vision, loss of coordination, amnesia and respiratory and cardiac failure. Long term damage may well result to brain, heart and sight and the hallucinogenic experience, although very powerful, may well be completely occluded from conscious recall. It seems really crazy that amongst all the herbs and hallucinogenic drugs, which the powers-that-be have declared as illegal, the undoubtedly dangerous plants like the daturas are not included. It makes you wonder at the logic behind their thinking processes. Reports of datura experiences published in websites, such as The Lycaeum, have predominantly 'bad trips' and warnings against the herb. When you consider that these accounts are from seasoned drug-users and psychonauts and not some Big Brother anti-drug propaganda campaign, it gives some idea of the scale of the danger potential of this plant and its poisons. I quote from one such account entitled 'Eye Paralysis' by an anonymous author and contributor to the Lycaeum Trip Reports:

I wouldn't do it again ... I wouldn't recommend it to anyone else either. The paralysis of vision was particularly disturbing as was the extreme constipation. On my scale of 1 to 10, I give this a 2, nutmeg was a 3, I hope never to experience a 1. There's a reason datura isn't popular and mainly that's because it sucks.

Finally, for the purpose of astrology and occult practices, the herbs of the genus *datura* are ruled by the planet Jupiter.

Torna Loca
Datura ceratocaula
Solanaceae

Torna loca means 'maddening plant' and here we have yet another very potent species of *datura* with all of the dangers of its close relatives. I have placed this one in a separate section because, apart from many similarities to the other species, this type is also very different in appearance and growing habitat. Torna loca is a fleshy almost succulent species and likes to grow in marshes or in shallow water. The seed-pods are also different as in this species they are smooth and devoid of the usual spines. Possibly it evolved this way because its more aquatic habitats offer it more protection. Torna loca grows in Mexico as well as other semi-tropical and tropical areas of the globe.

This herb was regarded by the ancient Aztecs as the 'Sister of Ololiuqui' (the entheogen *Turbina corymbosa* covered elsewhere) and was thought of as a holy medicine to be reverently addressed before use. It is significant to note that the Aztecs thought of the plant spirit as feminine in nature, seeing as daturas and other tropane-containing herbs related to them are often thought of as some of the 'femme fatales' of the plant kingdoms. Indeed, they are very beautiful, very enchanting and very deadly!

V

Vanilla Cactus
Cereus grandiflorus
Cactaceae
Other common names: Night Blooming Cereus, Large-flowered
Cactus, Sweet-scented Cactus

The vanilla cactus is a sprawling fleshy plant with long branching cylindrical stems covered with small spines. It bears large white flowers, which can be as much as 12in. across and which emit a strong vanilla-scented perfume, hence one of its names. These magnificent blossoms are produced at the ends of stems and at the sides and emerge from the clusters of spines. They open in the evening and only stay this way for about 6 hours, which in the natural habitat is time enough for them to get pollinated. After flowering, an acidic orange-red egg-shaped fruit is produced resembling a huge gooseberry in many ways. The vanilla cactus is found growing in Mexico, the West Indies, other tropical parts of America and in Naples.

The young stems and flowers are harvested in July and these contain a milky acrid latex. The cactus has sedative and diuretic properties as well as being a cardiac stimulant. It has been used as a substitute for the herbal heart-drug digitalis. In large doses, besides causing digestive and gastric disturbance it also produces delirium and hallucinations. Some related species of *Cereus* are reported to contain phenethylamines, although the alkaloids responsible for the vanilla cactus's effects are not known.

Voacanga
Voacanga africana
Apocynaceae

Voacanga is an evergreen tree found growing naturally in the

West-African rainforests. It reaches 20ft. or more and bears broad oval leaves some 5 or 6in. in length. The fruit of the tree is a berry, which contains several irregularly-shaped brown seeds. The seed cluster can be readily likened to the appearance of a brain. Voacanga is both drought and frost tender and likes a rich soil and a semi-shaded growing position. Propagation is from cuttings or seed and it has been found that fresh seed is far more likely to have a successful germination rate.

The voacanga tree has been until recently one of the closely guarded secrets of the African shamans. It is said that they ingest the root and trunk bark as a cerebral stimulant and take the seeds for visionary experiences. The stimulation resulting from voacanga ingestion increases endurance and at higher levels of dosage leads to hallucinogenic experiences. Voacanga is held in very high esteem as a sacred herb used in rituals and shamanic ceremonies.

It is a close relative of *Tabernanthe iboga*, detailed earlier on as the source of the powerful alkaloid ibogaine. The seeds of voacanga contain up to 10% indole alkaloids, including voacamine and voacangine and these substances are found at lower concentrations in the bark of the tree.

Y

Yohimbe
Pausinystalia yohimbe (Syn. Corynanthe yohimbe)
Rubiaceae
Other common names: Lizard Tail, Yerba del Pasmo, Yerba Mansa

Yohimbe is a tropical evergreen tree from the same family as coffee *(Caffea arabica)* and is becoming increasingly well known due to its reported and actual aphrodisiac properties. It bears oval leaves about 4in. long and the flowers make way for seeds carried in paper-thin winged foils. The yohimbe tree is frost and drought tender and likes a rich soil with plenty of humus. It dislikes being in full sun. Yohimbe grows in the West-African rainforests of the Cameroons, Congo and parts of Nigeria. Propagation is by seed or cuttings, though both methods can be difficult. The seeds lose their viability very quickly so must be fresh and the tree needs warmth to germinate and grow.

At this point, it seems the correct place to include an 'Important Conservation Notice', from Torsten Wiedemann:

This species (Yohimbe) is the only commercial source of the drug yohimbine. European and American pharmaceutical companies are purchasing hundreds of tons of bark every year, which comes from tens of thousands of mature trees. This is a rainforest tree of a population density of about 5 trees per hectare and it is almost at the verge of extinction in the wild due to poor government controls and lack of restraint by the pharmaceutical companies. The raw bark costs less than 1 US dollar per kilo from the harvesters and is resold in the West for the incredible profit of several thousand percent. Only one government has started to establish plantations but they are still many years from producing the needed quantities. In the meantime the destruction goes on, which

119

will see this species virtually eliminated from its native habitat. We urge that anyone contemplating the purchase of any yohimbe product should make enquiries as to whether it is plantation grown. The environmentally responsible façade of the pharma companies is not to be trusted unless they clearly state that it is plantation sourced rather than the so-called 'responsibly and sustainably harvested' material.

Once again we are reminded that many of the sacred herbs are under threat of extinction in the wild and that conservation should be a far greater priority than some attempt to get high!

Author Peter Stafford, in his entheobotanical classic *Psychedelics Encyclopedia,* reports that the drug yohimbine is also present in other species of its genus to varying degrees, as well as being found in *Aspidosperma quebranchoblanco* and *Mitragyna stipulosa.*

Yohimbe can be prepared as a stimulating tea by boiling 6–10 teaspoons of the bark shavings in a pint of water for 5 minutes and letting this cool. The brew should also be strained before drinking. Adding a gram of Vitamin C will help reduce potential nausea and potentiate the effects. Honey may be added to sweeten the unpleasant and bitter taste. After about 30 minutes, warm shivers may be experienced going up the spine and also mild restlessness and an anxious feeling may accompany this. Very soon this should be replaced with a pleasant euphoric and relaxed state of intoxication lasting several hours with noticeably enhanced sexual receptiveness and sensitivity as well as increased ability to perform. The indole alkaloid yohimbine acts by dilating the blood vessels in the lower abdomen and genital area and thereby causes stronger erectile ability in men and increased genital stimulation in women. Larger doses can be hallucinogenic but also very unpleasant and dangerously toxic. Even at lower doses it is wise to be aware that yohimbine is a monoamine oxidase inhibitor and, therefore, should not be ingested internally along with any of a long list of foods and drinks and drugs. Failure to pay attention to this caution may well result in violent headaches, sickness, blood-pressure crises, heart problems and death, in some cases. Monoamine oxidase acts as a monitor and chemical control over enzyme balance in the body but when it is inhibited it can potentiate the hallucinogenic and psychoactive effects of herbal preparations that have been ingested. Unfortunately, and if we are unwise, it can also potentiate harmful physiological changes and symptoms of danger. The list of things that needs to be avoided before using yohimbe is given below: alcohol, antihistamines, amphetamines, tranquilisers and sedatives, avocados, ripe bananas, broad beans, Ecstasy (drug), pickled herring and kippers, yeast extracts, mescaline, macromerine, nutmeg, mature cheese, caffeine, preserved figs, chicken liver, chocolate, cocoa, sauerkraut, liquorice, narcotics, ephedrine and oils of dill, parsley and fennel. Whilst you may enjoy improving your sex-life with the use of yohimbe, it is still better to be safe than sorry in more ways than one!

Bibliography and Further Recommended Reading

Adovasio, J.M., and Fry, G.F., 1976. 'Prehistoric Psychotropic Drug Use in Northeastern Mexico and Trans-Pecos Texas'. EB 30 / 1, 94-96

Agrippa, H.C., 1651. *Three Books of Occult Philosophy.* trans. J. French, Moule, London.

Allen, B., 2000. *Last of the Medicine Men.* BBC Publishing, London.

Allen, J.W., and Merlin, M.D., Observations regarding the Suspected Psychoactive Properties of Paneolus Foenisecii Maire by John W. Allen and Mark D. Merlin. *Mushroom John's Shroom World.*

Andrews, Steve and Katrinia Rindsberg, 2010. *Herbs of the Northern Shaman,* O-Books, Winchester UK, Washington USA.

Balick, M.J., and Cox, P.A., 1996. *Plants, People and Culture: The Science of Ethnobotany.* Scientific American Library, New York.

Blackwood, B., 1940. 'Use of Plants Among the Kukukuku of South-East Central New Guinea', 111-126 in *Proceedings of the Sixth Pacific Science Congress.* Vol.4, California.

Brunton, R., 1989. *The Abandoned Narcotic: Kava and Cultural Instability in Melanesia.* Cambridge University Press, Cambridge.

Burton-Bradley, B.G., 1972. 'Betel Chewing', 66-67in P.Ryan (Ed.) *The Encyclopedia of Papua and New Guinea. Vol. 1,* Melbourne University Press, Carlton, Victoria.

Bye, R.A., Jnr. 1979. 'Hallucinogenic Plants of the Tarahumara'. *J. Ethnopharmacology., 1,* 23-48.

Campbell, T.N., 1958. Origin of the Mescal Bean Cult. *Am. Anthrop., 60,* 156-160

Castaneda, C., 1974. *The Teachings of Don Juan.* Simon and Schuster, Pocket Books, New York.

Culpeper, N., 1805. *The English Physician and Complete Herbal.*

Lewis and Roden, London.

Culpeper, N., (Ed.) D. Potterton, 1983. *Culpeper's Colour Herbal.* W.Foulsham & Company Limited, Slough, Berks., UK.

De Korne, J., 1994. *Psychedelic Shamanism: The Cultivation, Preparation and Shamanic Use of Psychotropic Plants.* Loompanics, Port Townsend, WA.

De Smet, P.A.G.M., 1996. 'Some Ethnopharmacological Notes on African Hallucinogens'. JEp 50 / 3, 141-46.

Diaz, Jose, L. et al., 1986. 'Psychopharmacologic Analysis of an Oneirogenic Plant: Calea zacatechichi'. *J. Ethnopharmacology,* v.18, 229-243.

Dobkin de Rios, M., 1974. 'The Influence of Psychotropic Flora and Fauna on Maya Religion'. CA 15 / 2, 147-64.

Emboden, W.A., 1978. 'The Sacred Narcotic Lily of the Nile: Nymphaea Caerulea'. EB 32 / 4, 395-407.

Emboden, W.A., 1979. *Narcotic Plants: Hallucinogens, Stimulants, Inebriants and Hypnotics, Their Origins and Uses.* Studio Vista, London.

Emboden, W.A., 1981. 'Transcultural Use of Narcotic Water Lilies in Ancient Egyptian and Maya Drug Ritual'. JEp 3, 39-83.

Emboden, W.A., Jr. 1979. *Narcotic Plants of the World.* Macmillan, New York.

Evans, W. C., 1979. 'Tropane Alkaloids of the Solanaceae'. 241-54 in J.G. Hawkes et al, *The Biology and Taxonomy of the Solanaceae.*

Fernandez, J.W., 1972. *'Tabernanthe iboga:* Narcotic Ecstasis and the Work of the Ancestors,' 237-60 in P.T. Furst (Ed.), *Flesh of the Gods.*

Fernandez, J.W., 1982. *Bwiti: An Ethnography of the Religious Imagination in Africa.* Princeton University Press, Princeton.

Furst, P.T., 1972. (Ed.) *Flesh of the Gods.* Praeger Publishers, New York.

Furst, P.T., 1974. Hallucinogens in pre-columbian art. *Spec. Publ. Mus. Texas Tech. Univ.,* 7 55-102

Furst, P.T., 1976. *Hallucinogens and Culture*. Chandler and Sharp Publishers, San Francisco.

Goodman, S.M. and Hobbs, J.J., 1988. 'The Ethnobotany of the Egyptian Eastern Desert: A Comparison of Common Plant Usage Between Two Culturally Distinct Bedouin Groups'. JEp 23 / 1, 73-89.

Grieve, Mrs. M., 1992. *A Modern Herbal*. Tiger Books International, London.

Guzman, G., 1983. *The Genus Psilocybe: A Systematic Revision of the Known Species Including the History, Distribution and Chemistry of the Hallucinogenic Species. Beihefte zur Nova Hedwigia Heft 74.* J.Kramer, Vaduz, Germany.

Guzman, G., 1995. 'Supplement to the monograph of the genus *Psilocybe'. Bibliotheca Mycologica*. 159: 91-141

Guzman, G. and S.H. Pollock., 1979. 'Tres nuevas especies y dos nuevas registros de los hongos alucinogenos en Mexico y datos sobre su cultivo en el laboratorio'. *Bol Soc Mex Mic* 13: 261-270

Harding, P., 1996. *Mushrooms and Toadstools Photoguide*. Harper Collins Publishers, Glasgow.

Harner, M.J., 1976 (Ed.) *Hallucinogens and Shamanism*. Oxford University Press, London.

Heim, R., 1958. 'Diagnose latine du *Psilocybe wassonii* Heim, espece hallucinogenedes Azteques'. *Revue de Mycologie* 23(1): 119-120.

Heim, R. and Wasson, R.G., 1958. *Les Champignons Hallucinogenes du Mexique. Etudes Ethnologiques, Taxinomiques, Biologiques, Physiologiques et Chimiques*. Archives du Museum National d'histoire Naturelle, Series 7, Vol. VI. Paris, France.

Heim, R. and Wasson, R.G., 1965. 'The "Mushroom Madness" of the Kuma'. BLMHU 21 / 1, 1-36.

Hoffer, A. and Osmond, H., 1967. *The Hallucinogens*. Academic Press, New York.

Hoffman, A., 1960. Die psychotroppen Wirkstoffe der

mexikanischen Zauberpilze. *Chimia, 14,* 309-318

Hoffman, A., 1961. Der Wirkstoffe der mexikanischen Zauberdroge Oloiuqui. *Planta medica. 9,* 354-367

Hoffman, A., 1964. *Die Mutterkornalkaloide.* Ferdinand Enke Verlag, Stuttgart.

Hoffman, A., 1968. Psychotomimetic agents. In Burger, A., (Ed.): *Chemical Constitution and Pharmacodynamic Action.* Vol. 2 169-235, M. Dekker, New York.

Hoogshagen, S., 1959. 'Notes on the sacred mushroom from Coatlan, Oaxaca, Mexico'. *Oklahoma Anthropological Society Bulletin* 7: 71-74

Johnston, T.F., 1972. *'Datura fastuosa:* Its Use In Tsonga Girls' Initiation'. EB 26 / 4, 340-51.

Icke, D., 1999. *The Biggest Secret.* Bridge of Love Publications, Scottsdale, AZ.

Krikorian, A.D., 1984. 'Kat and Its Use: An Historical Perspective'. JEp 12 / 2, 115-78.

Lebot, V., Merlin, M. and Lindstrom, L., 1992. *Kava The Pacific Drug.* Yale University Press, New Haven.

Lehane, B., 1977. *The Power of Plants.* McGraw-Hill Book Co. (UK) Ltd., Maidenhead.

Lipp, F.J., 1985. 'Mixe ritual: an ethnographic and epigraphical comparison'. *Mexicon* 7: 83-87. Berlin.

Lipp, F.J., 1990. 'Mixe concepts and uses of entheogenic mushrooms'. In: Riedlinger, T.J., (Ed.) *The Sacred Mushroom Seeker: Essays for R. Gordon Wasson.* Ethnomycological Studies No. 11, pp. 151-159. Discorides Press, Portland, OR.

Lipp, F.J., 1991. *The Mixe of Oaxaca: Religion, Ritual and Healing.* Foreword by M. S. Edmondson, pp. ix-ix. University of Texas Press, Austin, TX.

Manniche, L., 1989. *An Ancient Egyptian Herbal.* University of Texas Press, Austin, TX.

McKenna, T., 1992. *Food of the Gods: The Search for the Original Tree of Knowledge.* Rider, London.

Merrill, W.L., 1977. *An Investigation of Ethnographic and Archaeological Specimens of Mescal beans (Sophora secundiflora) in American Museums.* Research Reports in Ethnobotany 1, Museum of Anthropology, University of Michigan, Ann Arbor.

Myerhoff, B.G., 1974. *Peyote Hunt: The Sacred Journey of the Huichol Indians.* Cornell University Press, Ithaca and London.

Negrin, J., 1975. *The Huichol Creation of the World,* E.B. Crocker Art Gallery, Sacramento.

Osmond, H., 1955. Ololiuqui: The Ancient Aztec Narcotic. Remarks on the effects of *Rivea corymbosa* (ololiuqui), *J. Ment. Sci., 101,* 526-537.

Ott, J., 1993. *Pharmacotheon: Entheogenic Drugs, Their Plant Sources and History,* Natural Products Co., Kennewick, WA.

Ott, J., 1995. *The Age of Entheogens/The Angel's Dictionary,* Natural Products Co., Kennewick, WA.

Ott, J., 1996. 'Entheogens II: On Entheology and Entheobotany', JPD 28 / 2, 205-9.

Ott, J., and Bigwood, J. (Ed.) 1978. *Teonanacatl: Hallucinogenic Mushrooms of North America.* Madrona Publishers, Seattle, Wash.

Poole, F.J.P., 1987. 'Ritual rank, the self and ancestral power: liturgy and substance in a Papua New Guinea society', 149-96 in L. Lindstrom (Ed.) *Drugs in Pacific Societies.*

Pope, H.G., Jr. 1969. *Tabernanthe iboga* – an African narcotic plant of social importance. *Econ. Bot., 23,* 174-184.

Powell, J.M., 1976. 'Ethnobotany', 106-183 in K. Paijmans (Ed.), *New Guinea Vegetation,* Elsevier, Oxford.

Raffauf, R.F., 1970. *A Handbook of Alkaloids and Alkaloid-Containing Plants,* Wiley Interscience, New York.

Reay, M., 1960. 'Mushroom Madness in the New Guinea Highlands', OCE 31, 137-39.

Riedlinger, T.J. (Ed.), 1960. *The Sacred Mushroom Seeker: Essays for R. Gordon Wasson,* Ethnomycological Studies No. 11,

Dioscorides Press, Portland, Oregon.

Rose, G., 1993. *The Psychedelics, Volume One: An A-Z of Psychedelics,* Sirius Publications.

Rose, G., 1993. *The Psychedelics, Volume Three: The Psychedelic Cacti,* Sirius Publications.

Rudgley, R., 1993. *The Alchemy of Culture: Intoxicants in Culture,* British Museum Press, London.

Rudgley, R., 1998. *The Encyclopedia of Psychoactive Substances,* Little, Brown and Company, London.

Safford, W.E., 1922. 'Daturas of the Old World and New: An Account of Their Narcotic Properties and Their Use in Oracular and Initiatory Ceremonies', 537-67 in Annual Report of the Smithsonian Institution 1920, Washington DC.

Savona, G. et al. 1979. Journal of the Chemical Society, Perkins Transactions 1: 643-646.

Savona, G. et al. 1979. Journal of the Chemical Society, Perkins Transactions 1: 533-534.

Schultes, R.E., 1940. 'Teonanacatl: The Narcotic Mushroom of the Aztecs', AA 42, 429-43.

Schultes, R.E., 1941. *A Contribution to Our Knowledge of Rivea Corymbosa, the Narcotic Ololiuqui of the Aztecs,* Harvard Botanical Museum, Cambridge, Mass.

Schultes, R.E., 1969. Hallucinogens of plant origin. *Science, 163,* 245-254.

Schultes, R.E., 1972. The utilisation of hallucinogens in primitive societies - use, misuse or abuse? In Keup, W. (Ed.): *Drug Abuse. Current Concepts and Research.* Charles C. Thomas, Springfield, Ill., 17-26.

Schultes, R.E., 1976. *Hallucinogenic Plants,* Golden Press, New York.

Schultes, R.E., 1977. 'The Botanical and Chemical Distribution of Hallucinogens', 25-55 in B.M. Du Toit (Ed.), *Drugs, Rituals and Altered States of Consciousness,* Balkema, Rotterdam.

Schultes, R.E. and Hofmann, A., 1980. *The Botany and Chemistry of Hallucinogens,* Second Edition, Charles C. Thomas, Springfield, Illinois.

Schultes, R.E. and Hofmann, A., 1992. *Plants of the Gods: Their Sacred, Healing and Hallucinogenic Powers,* Healing Arts Press, Rochester, Vermont.

Shulgin, A.T., Sargent, T., and Naranjo, C., 1967. The Chemistry and Pharmacology of Nutmeg and Several Related Phenylisopropylamines. In Efron, D.H., Holmstedt, B., and Kline, N.S., (Eds.): *Ethnopharmacological Search for Psychoactive Drugs. Public Health Serv. Publ. No. 1645,* 202-214.

Siebert, D, (7 Nov, 2,000. – Version 1.68, Last update). *The Salvia divinorum FAQ.* Available: http://salvia.lycaeum.org/faq.html (11 Nov, 2,000).

Stafford, P., 1977. *Psychedelics Encyclopedia,* And / Or Press, Berkeley, CA.

Wasson, R.G., 1958. The divine mushroom: primitive religion and hallucinatory agents. *Proc. Am. Phil. Soc. 102,* 221-223.

Wasson, R.G., 1962. The hallucinogenic mushrooms of Mexico and psilocybin: a bibliography. *Bot. Mus. Leafl., Harvard Univ., 20,* 20-73.

Wasson, R.G., et al., 1974. *Maria Sabina and Her Mazatec Mushroom Velada,* Ethnomycological Studies No. 3, Harcourt Brace Jovanovich, New York.

Weil, A.T., 1977. 'The Use of Psychoactive Mushrooms in the Pacific Northwest: An Ethnopharmacologic Report', BMLUH 25/5, 131-49.

Weil, A.T., 1979. 'Nutmeg as a Psychoactive Drug', 188-201in Efron et al, (Eds.), *Ethnopharmacologic Search for Psychoactive Drugs.*

Weir, S., 1985. *Qat in Yemen: Consumption and Social Change,* British Museum Publications, London.

Wiedemann, T, *Shaman Australis Botanicals* (Homepage of Shaman Australis Botanicals), Available: http://www.shaman-australis.com.au/shop/.

Wren, R.C., F.L.S., 1973. *Potter's New Encyclopedia of Botanical Drugs and Preparations,* Health Science Press, Wellingborough, Northants.

Wright, M., 1984. *The Complete Handbook of Garden Plants,* Michael Joseph / The Rainbird Publishing Group Limited, London.

Glossary of Medical Terminology

Acid: the opposite of alkali, having a sour taste and the ability to neutralize alkalis as well as having potential corrosive properties.

Alkali: a chemical substance that neutralises and is neutralized by acids.

Alkaloid: a nitrogen-containing constituent of a plant or herb, usually with powerful medicinal or pharmacological properties.

Allergy: excessive sensitivity to a substance.

Amine: a naturally occurring body chemical produced in response to emotion, fear and exercise.

Amino acid: an organic acid and a constituent of protein. It is derived from ammonia.

Ammonia: a colourless gas with a pungent smell and alkaline properties.

Amphetamine: a synthetic stimulant and decongestant drug.

Anaemia: too few healthy red blood cells or too little haemoglobin in these cells.

Anaesthetic: causes numbness and lack of sensitivity to pain.

Analgesic: drug that relieves or eradicates pain.

Antacid: neutralizes acid.

Antibacterial: destroys bacteria or inhibits their growth.

Antibiotic: inhibits growth of germs or kills them.

Antidote: a medicine taken to counteract a poison.

Anthelmintic: a worm-killer.

Antihistamine: prevents histamine, a body chemical which dilates the smallest blood vessels, constricts the muscle surrounding bronchial tubes and stimulates stomach secretions.

Antioxidant: prevents oxidation (combining with oxygen).

Antiseptic: prevents or inhibits the growth of germs.

Antispasmodic: helps to reduce spasms and seizures.

Aphrodisiac: arouses or enhances instinctive sexual desires.

Aromatic: with a spicy fragrance and stimulant properties.

Artery: blood vessel carrying blood away from the heart.

Asthma: disease of the respiratory system, characterized by wheezing and breathing difficulties. It is caused by bronchial spasms and may be due to an allergic reaction to various stimuli or caused by other factors.

Astringent: shrinks tissues and prevents the secretion of fluids.

Bacteria: microscopic germs that are different from viruses. Some bacteria are beneficial to health and others cause diseases to occur.

Bitters: tonic or medicine with a bitter flavouring.

Bronchial: of the air-carrying tubes in the lungs and chest.

Bronchitis: inflammation of the breathing-tubes in the chest.

Carcinogen: a substance able to cause cancer.

Cardiac: pertaining to the heart.

Catarrh: inflammation of the mucous membranes of nose and throat.

Cerebral: of the brain.

Chronic: a long-standing diseased condition.

Conjunctivitis: inflammation of the outer membranes of the eye.

Convulsion: a violent uncontrollable spasm.

Cyanogenic glycoside: a sugar that can be used to produce the toxin cyanide.

Cystitis: inflammation of the urinary system and bladder.

Decongestant: a drug used to relieve congestion, especially of the respiratory system.

Delerium: mental disturbance with hallucinations, agitation and incoherence.

Dermatitis: skin inflammation or irritation.

Digestive: pertaining to the digestion.

Diuretic: causing an increased flow of urine.

Dosage: amount of a medicine to be taken for a specific complaint or amount of a substance required to produce an effect.

Eczema: non-contagious skin disease, often with redness, irritation and scaling. It may be caused by an allergic reaction.

Emetic: used to cause vomiting.

Emphysema: a lung disease.

Enteritis: disease of the intestines.

Epilepsy: symptom or disease characterised by brain disturbance causing convulsions and loss of consciousness.

Essential oils: the same as volatile oils. Such oils evaporate at room temperature.

Expectorant: removes secretions from the bronchial tubes.

Extract: solution prepared by soaking a herb in solvent and then evaporating the liquid to concentrate it.

Fatigue: weariness after exertion, a general reduction of the efficiency of the body and its organs.

Flatulence: distension of the stomach and intestines due to accumulated gases.

Gastritis: inflammation of the stomach.

Genito-urinary disease: disease of the male or female genital and urinary organs.

Gingivitis: gum disease, characterised by inflammation, swelling and a readiness to bleed.

Gland: group of specialised cells that manufacture and secrete materials not required for their own needs.

Glycoside: a chemical compound that yields sugar and other substances by hydrolysis.

Gout: disease characterized by inflammation of the joints, especially the big toe.

Haemoglobin: iron-based pigment necessary for the transportation of oxygen by the red blood cells.

Haemorrhage: excessive bleeding.

Hallucinogen: substance that produces hallucinations – apparent sensual experiences that do not exist for other people.

Hepatic: pertaining to the liver.

Herb: plant valued for its medicinal properties, or for its aroma or taste.

Histamine: body chemical that causes tissue constriction and dilates small blood vessels. This can lead to leakage of fluid to form a rash or irritation.

Homeopathy: practice of introducing minute doses of a substance to cause the same symptoms as a disease that is being treated. Homeopaths acknowledge no diseases, only symptoms displayed by the body.

Hormone: chemical substance produced by the endocrine glands – the thymus, pituitary, thyroid, parathyroid, adrenal, ovaries, testes and pancreas. These substances regulate body functions and maintain balance.

Hydrolysis: decomposition by a chemical reaction with water.

Hyperacidity: excessive acid, especially in the stomach.

Hypertension: high blood pressure.

Hypnotic: producing sleep.

Hypotension: low blood pressure.

Hysteria: state of uncontrolled excessive excitement, a neurotic condition with possible anaesthesia and convulsions.

Insecticide: insect killer.

Irritant: causes irritation.

Impotence: lack of ability of a male to achieve or maintain erection of the penis.

Insomnia: inability to sleep.

Jaundice: symptomatic disease of the liver, due to damage to the organ, obstruction of bile production or destruction of red blood cells. It is characterized by yellowing of the skin and whites of the eyes.

Laryngitis: inflammation of the larynx, the cavity in the throat containing the vocal chords.

Laxative: a substance that stimulates bowel movement.

Libido: sex drive.

Lymph glands: glands located in the lymph vessels of the body.

These glands act to trap foreign and infectious material.

Mania: mental derangement with excessive excitement and possible violence.

Metabolism: chemical and physical processes in the maintenance of life of the body.

Mg: abbreviation for milligram, one-thousandth of a gram.

Migraine: periodic severe headaches, possibly accompanied by visual disturbance, nausea, vomiting and sensitivity to lights.

Monoamine oxidase: an enzyme, which assists in the breakdown of amines in the body.

Monoamine oxidase inhibitor: a substance that blocks the action of monoamine oxidase and may give rise to adverse effects. A monoamine oxidase inhibitor may also impede or stop the action of other vital enzymes.

Mucilage: gelatinous substance containing protein.

Narcosis: state of stupor produced by narcotic drug.

Narcotic: drug or substance that produces stupor and deadens pain. Narcotics tend to be addictive. They act by depressing the central nervous system and, in so doing, producing both drowsiness and euphoria.

Nervine: a drug that helps restore the nerves to a healthy state.

Neuralgia: intense intermittent pain caused by inflammation of face or head.

Opthalmic: of the eye.

Oxidation: combining a substance with oxygen.

Palpitations: rapid heartbeat.

Parasite: an animal or plant drawing nutriment directly from another species of life.

Pelvis: basin-like cavity in the area of the kidneys.

Parkinson's Disease: a progressive degenerative disease of the nervous system with tremor, muscular rigidity and emaciation.

Pharyngitis: inflammatory disease of the pharynx or throat area.

Poultice: material held between cloth or muslin to provide heat and moisture to an area of the body's surface. Poultices contain an active substance or substances plus a base to hold it all together. They are applied when hot and removed when cool.

Prostate: gland in the male surrounding the neck of the bladder and urethra. In older men it has a tendency to become infected, obstructed or cancerous.

Psoriasis: chronic skin disease with patches of flaking skin.

Psychedelic: expanding the mind's awareness.

Psychoactive: affecting the mental state in some fashion.

Psychonaut: a voyager into the mind's capabilities, an explorer of the mind, possibly with the aid of hallucinogenic drugs or other shamanic practices. Just as an astronaut explores outer space a psychonaut does the same for the inner worlds.

Psychosis: mental disorder with altered reality states or personality changes for the sufferer, often with hallucinations and delusions.

Pulmonary: of the lungs.

Purgative: a powerful laxative, causing evacuation of the bowels.

Pyelitis: inflammation of the renal pelvis.

Relaxant: a substance, which has a calming effect similar to a tranquiliser.

Renal: of the kidneys.

Resin: a complex chemical substance that is usually hard, transparent or translucent in nature and which can produce effects on the human body.

Saponin: chemicals found in plants that may cause a toxic reaction. Saponins often produce a soapy lather in water.

Sedative: reduces anxiety and restlessness and aids sleep.

Soporific: produces sleep or drowsiness.

Stimulant: stimulates activity of body organs and produces short-term energy.

Stomachic: promotes constriction of the stomach muscles.

Styptic: helps to stop bleeding.

Sudorific: increases sweat production.

Syphilis: a contagious venereal disease.

Tannins: complex acidic mixtures of chemicals found in plants.

Terpenes: complex hydrocarbons. Most volatile oils are terpenes.

Tincture: solution of chemicals in an alcoholic solvent.

Tinnitus: persistent ringing in the ears.

Tonic: medicinal preparation to promote and restore well-being.

Toxin: a poison.

Tranquilizer: a substance that reduces anxiety and calms a person who is disturbed.

Tryptophan: a certain class of amino acid.

Tyramine: a chemical component of the body, which at normal levels helps maintain a healthy blood pressure. In the presence of some drugs, such as monoamine oxidase-inhibitors, tyramine can rise to unacceptable levels, which can be toxic or even fatal.

Venereal disease: a disease spread by sexual intercourse.

Virus: infectious organism that reproduces itself within the cells of its host.

Volatile oils: see **Essential oils**.

Water-soluble: able to be dissolved in water.

Glossary of Botanical Terms

Acrid: leaving a burning sensation in the mouth when chewed or otherwise tasted.

Annual: a plant that completes its growth in one year.

Anthers: the part of the stamen containing pollen.

Aromatic: having a more or less agreeable odour.

Auriculate: with ear-like lobes (usually small) at the base.

Alternate: staggered singly around a stem.

Axil: upper angle between a leaf or bract and a stem.

Berry: a soft fruit containing the seeds in pulp.

Biennial: a plant that completes its growth in two years, usually flowering in the second.

Bract: a leaf-like organ, often coloured and supporting a flower.

Bulb: a bulb is more or less globular and consists of fleshy scales or modified leaves. It is often formed underground.

Calyx: cup-like organ housing the flower.

Campanulate: bell-shaped.

Cordate: heart-shaped.

Corolla: the petals of a flower considered as a whole.

Cyme: an inflorescence where the primary axis bears a single terminal flower which develops first.

Deciduous: falling off, usually of a plant, tree or shrub that loses its leaves in the autumn.

Entheobotanical: pertaining to the study of sacramental plants and those used for shamanic purposes.

Entheogen: literally means 'becoming divine within'. Commonly used to denote a psychoactive herb or substance, especially those with hallucinogenic properties.

Flowerhead: an arrangement of flowers in a group, often surrounded by rows of bracts.

Hermaphrodite: possessing both male and female functional reproductive organs.

Inflorescence: flower cluster including the stem, flowers and bracts.

Invasive: having a tendency to invade or encroach upon new land or territory.

Lanceolate: lance-shaped.

Latex: a white or yellowish milky sap.

Ovate: egg-shaped.

Perennial: a plant that lives for more than two years and flowers each year.

Rhizome: an underground stem, usually perennial.

Rib: the central part or vein of a leaf.

Semi-aquatic: growing partially in water, amphibious in nature.

Spadix: a spike of flowers.

Stamen: the male reproductive part of a flower bearing pollen.

Tubercule: a small projection or possibly wart-like excrescence or a very small tuber.

Umbel: an inflorescence with all the flower stalks arising from a single main point. The outer flowers open first.

Index

All common names are in bold type and botanical ones are in italics.

MOON

BOOKS

PAGANISM & SHAMANISM

What is Paganism? A religion, a spirituality, an alternative belief system, nature worship? You can find support for all these definitions (and many more) in dictionaries, encyclopaedias, and text books of religion, but subscribe to any one and the truth will evade you. Above all Paganism is a creative pursuit, an encounter with reality, an exploration of meaning and an expression of the soul. Druids, Heathens, Wiccans and others, all contribute their insights and literary riches to the Pagan tradition. Moon Books invites you to begin or to deepen your own encounter, right here, right now.

If you have enjoyed this book, why not tell other readers by posting a review on your preferred book site.

Recent bestsellers from Moon Books are:

Journey to the Dark Goddess
How to Return to Your Soul
Jane Meredith
Discover the powerful secrets of the Dark Goddess and
transform your depression, grief and pain into healing
and integration.
Paperback: 978-1-84694-677-6 ebook: 978-1-78099-223-5

Shamanic Reiki
Expanded Ways of Working with Universal Life Force Energy
Llyn Roberts, Robert Levy
Shamanism and Reiki are each powerful ways of healing; together,
their power multiplies. *Shamanic Reiki* introduces techniques to
help healers and Reiki practitioners tap ancient healing wisdom.
Paperback: 978-1-84694-037-8 ebook: 978-1-84694-650-9

Pagan Portals – The Awen Alone
Walking the Path of the Solitary Druid
Joanna van der Hoeven
An introductory guide for the solitary Druid, *The Awen Alone* will
accompany you as you explore, and seek out your own place
within the natural world.
Paperback: 978-1-78279-547-6 ebook: 978-1-78279-546-9

A Kitchen Witch's World of Magical Herbs & Plants
Rachel Patterson
A journey into the magical world of herbs and plants, filled with
magical uses, folklore, history and practical magic. By popular
writer, blogger and kitchen witch, Tansy Firedragon.
Paperback: 978-1-78279-621-3 ebook: 978-1-78279-620-6

Medicine for the Soul
The Complete Book of Shamanic Healing
Ross Heaven
All you will ever need to know about shamanic healing and how to
become your own shaman...
Paperback: 978-1-78099-419-2 ebook: 978-1-78099-420-8

Shaman Pathways – The Druid Shaman
Exploring the Celtic Otherworld
Danu Forest
A practical guide to Celtic shamanism with exercises and
techniques as well as traditional lore for exploring the Celtic
Otherworld.
Paperback: 978-1-78099-615-8 ebook: 978-1-78099-616-5

Traditional Witchcraft for the Woods and Forests
A Witch's Guide to the Woodland with Guided Meditations and
Pathworking
Mélusine Draco
A Witch's guide to walking alone in the woods, with guided
meditations and pathworking.
Paperback: 978-1-84694-803-9 ebook: 978-1-84694-804-6

Wild Earth, Wild Soul
A Manual for an Ecstatic Culture
Bill Pfeiffer
Imagine a nature-based culture so alive and so connected,
spreading like wildfire. This book is the first flame...
Paperback: 978-1-78099-187-0 ebook: 978-1-78099-188-7

Naming the Goddess
Trevor Greenfield
Naming the Goddess is written by over eighty adherents and
scholars of Goddess and Goddess Spirituality.
Paperback: 978-1-78279-476-9 ebook: 978-1-78279-475-2

Shapeshifting into Higher Consciousness
Heal and Transform Yourself and Our World with Ancient
Shamanic and Modern Methods
Llyn Roberts
Ancient and modern methods that you can use every day to
transform yourself and make a positive difference in the world.
Paperback: 978-1-84694-843-5 ebook: 978-1-84694-844-2

Readers of ebooks can buy or view any of these bestsellers by
clicking on the live link in the title. Most titles are published in
paperback and as an ebook. Paperbacks are available in traditional
bookshops. Both print and ebook formats are available online.

Find more titles and sign up to our readers' newsletter at
http://www.johnhuntpublishing.com/paganism
Follow us on Facebook at https://www.facebook.com/MoonBooks
and Twitter at https://twitter.com/MoonBooksJHP

Printed and bound by PG in the USA

USA2019PGIL